Discover

The

MacMillan Way

Journal of the people, places and histories discovered
when walking the 290 miles of the MacMillan Way
from Boston to Chesil Beach

Keith Pauling

ISBN 978-1-291-60910-3

By the same author

Discovering the Thames Pathway (2009)

Discovering the Dales Way (2010)

Discovering the Cotswolds Way (2012)

Discovering the MacMillan Way (2013)

View the website for Thames Pathway

www.thamespathway.com

DEDICATION

Dedicated to MacMillan Cancer Support

All royalties will be donated to MacMillan Cancer Support

Direct donations can be made to

MacMillan Cancer Support
89 Albert Embankment
London
SE1 7UQ

MAP OF THE MACMILLAN WAY

Boston

Birmingham

Spalding

Oakham • • Stamford

Norwich

■ Northampton

Epwell ■ Flore

Stow on the Wold

■ Oxford

■ Cirencester
Tetbury

■ Bradford on Avon

London

■ Castle Cary

Southampton

■ Sherborne

Abbotsbury

INTRODUCTION

The 290 mile Macmillan Way is a long distance footpath that was developed to raise public awareness of the charity "Macmillan Cancer Support". The charity provides much-needed support for those afflicted by this terrible illness and also general assistance for their families. In buying this book you have already made a donation to this most worthy cause.

This is my fourth long distance walk on my long-term mission to discover the joys of the British countryside. The Thames Path (180 miles), the Dales Way (84 miles) and the Cotswold Way (104 miles) have all been previously covered. The Macmillan Way will be the longest expedition yet at a distance of 290 miles. That is not counting all of the many diversions and distractions that will occur while I have a "poke around" at all of the interesting things that I stumble across on my journey.

The line of the MacMillan Way can be looked at in several different ways. In a simple map interpretation the path runs from around the middle of the east coast of England to the middle of the south coast. In so doing it cuts away the south east commuter-belt corner of the country.

Geologically speaking the route mostly follows a great ridge of oolitic limestone that passes through the middle of England. This sedimentary rock has some subtle differences in colour at different locations, but it can generally be considered to be of a toffee or honey tone. It is from this stone that the distinctive cottages of the Cotswolds are constructed. The complete Jurassic limestone belt starts in South Yorkshire and extends to the south coast.

On a scenic basis the full route of the Macmillan Way links a delightful series of quintessential English towns and villages. The Jurassic stone gives them a commonality, but each one has developed its own distinctive charms. The Georgian grandeur of Stamford, the tightly knit Cotswold market town of Stow-on-the-Wold and the bustling activity of Bradford on Avon provide different urban backdrops. When it comes to the smaller villages it is hard to know where to start. The delights of Lower Slaughter, Castle Combe and Abbotsbury are all well known, but there are equal delights waiting to be discovered in the relatively more obscure settlements of Ratley, Sherston and Yetminster among many others.

The Macmillan Way makes good use of several sections of other established long distance pathways. The Cleveland Way, Viking Way, Jurassic Way, D'Arcy Dalton Way, Leland Trail and Monarchs Way will all be utilised at some point. The Macmillan Way also connects to other major long-distance paths such as the Thames Path and the South West Coast Path.

I am going to encounter many long sections of unspoiled farmland. Starting off with the flat areas of the fens, the Macmillan Way will take me through many, many fields of arable crops and pastures. At times the ubiquitous oil seed rape will seem to be taking over the world. I will prove for myself you that you will never know how wet you can possibly become until you have waded through shoulder-high rapeseed immediately after a cloudburst. The farming landscape will change when I arrive at the upland areas of the Cotswold Hills, and then transform again into the great parkland estates of Gloucestershire and Wiltshire. Eventually the path will take me across the Dorset Downs, where the cattle and sheep graze contentedly on the rich grass pastures.

The MacMillan Way travels through many different types of woodland areas. At first, in the fenlands, the trees are sparse to non-existent. Anything much taller than a bush stands out for miles during the first few hours of the walk. Later on I will encounter long stretches of path that twist and turn underneath broadleaved overhanging branches. There are numerous secret hidden sunken pathways in the woods. Some are a sheer pleasure to walk through while others will thrust me into an energy-sapping struggle through ankle-deep glutinous goo. On reaching Gloucestershire the path passes through the woodland to end all woodlands in the form of the absolutely majestic National Arboretum at Westonbirt.

The rivers change in an odd way. They tend to become smaller as the path progresses. In the beginning there are the extremely wide fenland giants of the River Witham and the River Welland. These two behemoths are followed by the arrow-straight channel of the River Glen that carries water draining from the Northamptonshire hills. After this, with the exception of a couple of miles of the Bristol Avon the waterways are all very much smaller. They twist and dart through gaps in the hills on their way to join their kindred spirits that make up the larger southern rivers. The Macmillan Way keeps mostly to their upper reaches and allows them to continue with their downstream journeys in solitude.

With plenty of open countryside at its disposal there is an abundance of wildlife to be seen along the Macmillan Way. There are so many birds along the fens it is impossible to estimate just how many there must be. All the way along the pathway the surrounding trees and hedgerows are alive with birds and the air is constantly filled with their songs. At various points I come across badger sets, catch a quick glimpse of a fox and on one memorable occasion I am fortunate enough to spot a deer standing alone in a glade in the woods.

The Macmillan Way will take me through areas which are soaked in our history. I discover where King John allegedly "lost" the crown jewels in The Wash and look down on the battlefield of Edgehill which marked the start of the treacherous blood-bath that was the English Civil War.

Early man makes a welcome and mysterious contribution too. From the ancient burial mounds to the haunting imagery of the Rollright Stones these mysterious landmarks cause me to ask many questions about the lives of our ancestors and their ways of seeing the world.

The Roman occupation is encountered many times. My travels take in the splendid excavated Roman Villa at Chedworth and the old Roman town now known as Cirencester. At frequent intervals the path both travels along and crosses several ancient Roman roads.

After the Romans left our shores the country slowly emerged from the Dark Ages and gave us the early Saxon settlements. The creation of the Godwin dynasty could have taught the Kennedy's a thing or two, or at least it could have done until it all came crashing down around them at Hastings with Harold on the receiving end of an eyeful of arrow. Other notable Saxons also cast their influence on the area and they will pop up from time to time. On a wide open hill in Somerset I will look around in awe and contemplate that I may truly be standing in the centre of ancient Camelot.

I will also be taking a look at some of the men and women who influenced the world that we currently live in. Where would we be today if it were not for the great statesmen, the writers, musicians and engineers? Their ingenuity and foresight has made a massive contribution to many things in our everyday lives that we all too often take for granted. On a pedestal high above them all stands the unparalleled genius that was the great Isambard Kingdom Brunel.

Join me on my journey through the English countryside. Together we will learn about the countryside, places and people along the Macmillan Way.

I hope you enjoy the book. Show your appreciation by making a difference to somebody worse off than yourself. Give a donation to Macmillan Cancer Support. Why not buy another copy to give to a friend? All profits go to the Macmillan charity.

BOSTON TO SURFLEET

DAY ONE
FIFTEEN MILES

Boston Stump

There is no difficulty at all in finding the starting point for this walk. Satellite navigation can safely be dispensed with and even the humble Ordnance Survey map is largely made redundant. As I gradually approach nearer to the town of Boston the distinctive tower of Boston Parish Church points 272 feet (83m) upwards into the sky providing a clear marker beacon from many miles away.

Ever since the time of its construction in the mid 15th century the tower of St. Botolph's Church has guided many people to the fenland town of Boston. It was not only of great benefit to the medieval traveller on foot or horseback. During the early years when Boston was one of England's busiest ports the "Stump" led a double life as a lighthouse. The upper level of the tower was used as a lantern during the hours of darkness to guide ships to the docks. In more recent times the clearly visible church tower provided a welcome navigation aid for British bomber pilots as they returned from their missions over Germany during the Second World War.

Officially the church bears the title of St. Botolph's Parochial Church of Boston but everyone simply refers to it as "Boston Stump". The exact origins of this colloquial term have disappeared over the years, but the probability must be that it alludes to the general shape of the spire-less tower.

St. Botolph's has the honour of being one of the largest Parish Churches in England. The nave measures 242 feet (74m) long and 104 feet (32m) wide. The construction of the church began in 1309 although the main body of the building was not finally completed until 1390. This seemingly lengthy building period was fairly common in those days. Churches were constructed taking meticulous care and skill with nothing being rushed. The tower itself was not started until 1450 and it was not finished until sometime between 1510 and 1520.

One of the more fascinating features of the church is the relationship between the structure of the building, the calendar and the clock. To start with there are 365 steps in the tower, corresponding to the number of days in the year. The relationship continues with twelve pillars (months) supporting the roof, seven doorways (days of the week) entering or leaving the building and fifty-two windows (weeks in the year) to provide light to the interior. To represent the clock there are twenty-four steps (hours in the day) leading up to the library and sixty steps (minutes in an hour) up to the roof.

A further feature of St. Botolph's is the collection of sixty-two misericords that can be found in the choir stalls. A misericord is a small carved ridge on the bottom of a tip-up wooden seat. When the seat is in the upright position the misericord forms a resting place upon which the weary can rest while still giving the outward appearance of standing. This must have come as a very welcome relief for many medieval choristers during long sessions of prayers! The misericords at St. Botolph's feature carvings that range widely in subject matter through heraldry, mythology and common everyday scenes. The carvings on these seats originate from 1390.

St. Botolph's sits on the east bank of the River Witham, just north of the town's Market Square. The area immediately around the church is pedestrianised with plenty of wooden benching available for those who wish to while away some time in the shadows of the medieval structure. No time for that for me because it is time to set off on my long trek towards the south coast.

Boston

Boston is one of those places which few people have probably actually been to. Unless there is a specific reason for visiting the town there is little chance that anyone would ever want to come here. It is not situated on the way to anywhere else either.

Geographically I had always thought that Boston was in the east of England so it surprised me to learn that Boston is in fact situated on the prime meridian, precisely 0 degrees east, 0 degrees west and due north of Greenwich. There is even a Meridian Road (PE21 0NB) that straddles the theoretical Greenwich meridian line.

The first thing that I come across is a fun fair in the Market Square. My visit coincides with the annual May Fair which has been a regular event during the first weekend of May since 1125. In those early days the fair would have been packed with merchants, tinkers, and peddlers. The attractions and entertainments would have included cock-fighting, archery and wrestling along with much feasting, drinking, music and general merry-making. The present-day attractions this early morning are standing still and silent, but no doubt in a few hours time their brightly coloured technology will be a flashing, whirling and stomach-churning delight to many. No doubt there will still be much eating, drinking, music and merry-making.

Rather like the roller-coaster rides of the visiting fun fair the town of Boston has had its share of ups and downs. If we turn to the first historical record that we can consider to be reasonably accurate, the Domesday Book of 1086, Boston does not even warrant a mention. At that time the settlement was officially recorded as Skirbeck in the Manor of Drayton.

Boston owes its early development and growth as a port to the great flood of 1014. Up until that point in time the River Witham flowed into the Wash at Drayton and this was the area that had been developed as a coastal port, with the River Witham providing a waterway access to Lincoln. Skirbeck was at that time situated on the Haven, which was then a tidal arm of The Wash. After the waters of the 1014 flood had subsided the geography of the area had been changed with the River Witham now linked up with The Haven. This new link provided for a far superior port than was previously available and the facilities at Drayton were gradually relocated to Skirbeck in order to gain from this advantage. At some stage in this transformation Skirbeck became renamed as Boston and has remained so ever since.

The origin of the town name is that it was probably named after St. Botolph being a corruption of "St. Botolph's Town". Botolph (or Botwulf) was an Early Saxon monk who died in 653. He was highly regarded as an early Saint of Travellers and his feast day was celebrated on June 17th. Botolph was very much revered throughout East Anglia as a man of great learning. At one time it was commonly thought that St. Botolph had founded a monastery at Boston, but scholars now accept that Botolph's monastery was located at Ikenoe in Suffolk. There can be little doubt that St. Botolph was very highly regarded due to the impressively large number of churches that were dedicated to him. Such churches are particularly prominent in the East Anglia region.

The port of Boston grew rapidly throughout the 12th and 13th centuries. Most of the export trade was principally made up of wool, supported by quantities of salt and lead. In return a wide range of goods were imported from Dutch and German trading ports.

The relationships between the trading ports of the North Sea helped to promote a heavy Dutch and Germanic influence on the people of Boston. This effect was particularly noticed during the various religious disputes that were regularly occurring at that time among many communities in England. The people were starting to rebel against what was considered to be the overbearing rule of the Church and many were turning towards the non-conformist styles of Christianity.

Boston gradually developed into a hot-bed of religious dispute and rebellion. Today we cannot imagine the pressures and stresses that this would have caused in the everyday lives of the people of the period. The local frictions came to a head in 1612 when John Cotton was appointed as the vicar of St. Botolph's. The Reverend Cotton preached a strong non-conformist message to his congregation. He further encouraged his parishioners, especially those for whom the local pressures were becoming too intense for comfort, to consider emigration to the new American colony of Massachusetts. John Cotton himself was later to follow his own advice and he emigrated to Massachusetts Bay in 1633. The vicar did not even have the inconvenience of changing his address when he arrived at his new home. Three years before John Cotton arrived in the New World the town of Boston Massachusetts had already been named in honour of their English ancestral home by his former parishioners.

The Boston that the early settlers to America left behind soon became embroiled with other more earthly problems. Plans were being drawn up to drain the fen lands in order for the landowners to gain more fertile land for farming. This did not go down very well with those traditional country folk who eked out their meagre living by exploiting the natural resources of the wetlands. A good example of this was the large number of people earning their daily crust from wildfowling. Supplying ducks and geese for meat and feathers was a major source of income for the local people and the drainage plans were understandably not entirely popular with them.

The combination of the religious and political unrest in the locality resulted in Boston being firmly on the Parliamentarian side during the Civil War. Many of the people of Boston considered that the war gave them a welcome side-effect. Lord Lindsey, who had been the major promoter of the fenland drainage scheme, was killed during one of the early battles of the war. Following the demise of its principal advocate the fenland drainage scheme was abandoned.

The drainage plan was resurrected during the second half of the eighteenth century. This time the scheme was implemented more effectively, resulting in thousands of acres of rich agricultural land being recovered for crop growing. Boston rapidly developed as the central hub of a thriving agricultural area.

At the same time as the land was being recovered a sluice was constructed across The Haven. The sluice enabled the build-up of silt in The Haven to be kept under control, allowing deeper drafted boats to use the docks. The fluctuating fortunes of Boston as a port began to rise again.

Over the last twenty years the fortunes of Boston have once more been on the decline. The relatively small docks are not as attractive to business as the larger container ports, and farming has not been a generator of great wealth. The demand for ever-lower labour costs has seen a great influx of immigrants into Boston, mainly from Eastern Europe. Today the immigrant population is reported as being as high as 25% of the total. Surveys have shown that Boston has one of the lowest proportions of "professional" occupations in the UK. With generally low wages and a lack of high earning professionals it is no great surprise that much of the town has a noticeable run-down feel to it.

Leaving the market square behind, the Macmillan Way leads me southwards out of Boston. My route crosses the River Witham and follows High Street South towards open country. I traverse a railway line at a level crossing. In my part of the world level crossings are a rarity so it is something of a novelty to negotiate the gates. Over the course of the next few days I will come across many similar crossings and the novelty will gradually wear off.

It is just after the level crossing that I came across a signpost that momentarily reminded me of the enormity of the task that lies before me. White raised lettering on a green background spelled out the stark message "MacMillan Way Abbotsbury 290 Miles". Oh well, as Confucius said, (or if he didn't he should have) "Even the longest journey starts with a single step".

The next bridge takes me over the South Forty Foot Drain. This waterway is one of the main fenland drainage channels and discharges its waters into the River Witham via the Black Sluice Pumping Station. The South Forty Foot Drain dates from 1635 and was part of the initial drainage work initiated by the aforementioned and unloved Lord Lindsey. In those days the channel was referred to as the "Lindsey Level". The Black Sluice Pumping Station was completed in 1946 and uses three large bore diesel pumps to discharge the waters of the drain into the River Witham.

I have now reached the point of no return. In front of me stretches the seemingly endless featureless salt marshes of The Wash. It will be ten miles before I so much as even see a proper road again. Once I set off from here I will be as isolated as I am ever going to be on this entire expedition. I do not know it yet, but this forthcoming section is going to turn into a real walk on the wild side.

The Salt Marshes

For the first two miles the Macmillan Way follows the right bank of The Haven in a southeast direction towards the sea. Most of the time I am walking along the flat top of an earth work sea bank which makes for an easy introduction to the trail. It would certainly be considerably more difficult if I had to pick my way through the marshy land that lay to either side of me.

There are a large number of squawking seagulls over to my right and the reason why they are there soon becomes evident. I have reached the Slippery Gowt refuse tip. The gulls are noisily circling whilst searching to pick out their next snack from among the mass of garbage deposited in the landfill. The name originates from a former Saxon sluice, now long gone. Gowt, being the Saxon name for a sluice, is an expression that I am going to become very familiar with over the next couple of days. After that it is very possible that I shall never hear the word mentioned again.

A little farther to my right I can just make out that there is another embankment. This must be the old Medieval Sea Bank and until the mid 19th century the fields between the two sea banks would have been occupied by untamed salt marshes. These have since been drained and successfully turned over to agriculture.

So far, so good, and I soon reach the four mile mark. At this point I leave the River Witham to continue on its final three miles to the sea through the final stretches of The Haven. My own route will travel around the edge of the salt marshes of The Wash to join up with the River Welland. Unfortunately for me it is not only the path that is changing direction, but so too is the weather.

So far the day has been decidedly chilly with some light rain. The morning weather forecast had promised that it would brighten up. How wrong could it be? The cold north-east wind is now really starting to bite. If that was not enough for me to contend with the drizzly rain is gradually turning into a chilly sleet. To rub it in even further I will also soon be on the receiving end of a vicious hailstorm. So much for the merry, merry month of May!

Every Sunday evening on "Countryfile" somebody, (usually John Craven), is banging on about the danger of global warming. I wish he was here with me today. We could have had a lively discussion about how this part of East Anglia was threatened by being scorched to a cinder. It would certainly distract our attention from the lashing winds and soaking rains.

Frampton Marsh

The last three miles have been completed in total solitude. There has not been a human being anywhere to be seen. Now there are several groups of people out on the marshes. All of them seem to be carrying some quite impressive observation equipment. I have arrived at Frampton Marsh. This is one of Britain's prime bird-watching centres and it is managed by the Royal Society for the Protection of Birds.

Frampton Marsh has much to commend itself for the twitching fraternity. It occupies most of the marshland between the River Witham and the River Welland, has over 3 km of well maintained footpaths and three excellent hides to enable the enthusiasts to find a position really close to the unsuspecting birds. There is also a well appointed visitor information centre packed with everything you could ever wish to know about the many species of fowl that can be seen here at different times of the year.

The feathery residents are mostly migratory, so there is a constant change to the balance of population throughout the year. Today there are Brent Geese everywhere, but this species will be almost completely gone by the end of the month. The Hen Harrier will likewise soon be on its migratory travels before returning to the marsh for the winter.

One of the great success stories of Frampton is facilitating the return of the Redshank to the area. The reserve now boasts over 200 mating pairs of Redshank, one of the highest population densities of this particular bird in the UK.

I have decided to keep my eyes keenly open in an attempt to spot an Avocet. This bird has a mostly white plumage with a black cap and wing trim. The Avocet's most distinctive feature is an upturned bill that enables the bird to efficiently gather up food from the shallow pools in which it wades. Fortunately the Avocet population at Frampton is sufficiently large to not prevent this particular novice from being able to put a tick against the bird within a short while.

The cold wind is really whipping across the marshes from the sea and consequently there are very few birds taking to the turbulent skies. Acrobatic displays by lapwings are definitely a non-starter today, and the skylarks are also keeping a low profile.

The furry creatures at Frampton are represented by hares, who are also keeping their heads down today. On brighter mornings it is not unusual to be able to observe these creatures indulging in one of the famous "boxing bouts" that are so often represented in pictures and sculptures.

I have now travelled more than eight miles from Boston and the distinctive outline of "The Stump" can still be seen even though the general visibility is poor. It truly is a great landmark out here, calling everyone from a very wide area towards the major settlement of the fens.

I must say that in these conditions the marshes possess a wild beauty which could not be experienced by the person who only dares to venture out in fine weather. The dark grey skies and gusting winds serve to highlight the isolation and desolation of these wetlands.

In bright calm conditions one would hardly notice that there is no shelter from the elements available out here. Bushes are a rarity and trees are non-existent. The only shelter from the wind that I managed to find was a small brick-built pumping station, and that was not much bigger than a garden shed. It was with some relief that I sat down on the leeward side of this welcome windbreak to partake of my sandwiches. I only wish that I had possessed the foresight to pack a flask of hot Bovril as well. I have walked several miles to get to Frampton Marsh, but anyone can access the visitor centre by car or bicycle from the main Spalding to Boston road. It is well worth parking the car and walking down the track to the sea wall to experience the marshes and the sense of wildness and isolation. I will certainly come back again at some point in the future.

The Tidal Welland

The River Welland is one of the major geographical features of the first few sections of the Macmillan Way. We are destined to meet each other on several occasions over the coming days. My first encounter with this waterway occurs almost exactly at the nine mile mark. The river will be on my left hand side for the next five miles until I reach Surfleet Seas End. My timing is such that the tide is running low so the river is not carrying much water, but the waters still remain impressively wide for an English River.

To the north east the river flows out into the Wash, but at over five miles away that is obviously too distant for me to be able to see. To the south west the water is flowing straight at me in a dead straight line. In the far distance I can make out a road bridge and it is with some astonishment that I realise from the map that this is two miles away. It is by far the highest object that I can detect at the moment. Boston Stump has by now been totally absorbed into the dark grey clouds.

Some of the statistics of the River Welland are quite thought provoking. In general terms the river is only 64 miles (105km) long, rising in the Hothorpe Hills near Sibertoft in Northamptonshire. However, when we look at the total catchment area of the river basin things start to take on a different appearance. The direct catchment area covers 609 square miles (1580 sq.km.) of which 179 square miles (460 sq.km.) are below sea level. Without the defensive embankments and the constant pumping out of surplus water this area would soon be flooded. Within the catchment area 257 miles (414 km.) are designated as being the main river, highlighting the contribution made by the tributaries to the major named waterway. The area drained by the River Welland is generally referred to as South Holland.

The earthwork embankments along both banks of the river are relatively high and from their elevated tops provide a good view across the fenland landscape. The rain has thankfully now stopped. Walking has become much easier with the wind blowing directly behind me and gently pushing me towards Fosdyke Bridge. I am now starting to notice more bushes appearing in view, with the occasional tree protruding from the fields to my right.

Fosdyke Bridge was visible from so far away that it seems to take forever before I eventually reach it, but in reality it was only a little over forty minutes. Fosdyke village has a population of around 500 people. A rather unusual piece of trivia is that Fosdyke is often categorised as being a coastal location because of the tidal nature of the river and the close proximity of The Wash. In fact The Wash used to be a lot closer to the village than it is now, and this provides me with a little gem of a story to include here.

Readers of my previous books will know that you can always rely on King John for a good story. King John can justifiably be considered to be one of our worst Kings. He was totally devious and usually behaved like a total and utter scoundrel. That said he can always be counted on to provide some interesting background stories and he now pops up once more to give us a bit of a laugh and at the same time cause us to wonder if he still managed to get one over on everyone.

In early October 1216 King John, accompanied by his retinue of royal servants and assorted hangers-on, travelled from Spalding, Lincolnshire to Bishop's Lynn (now known as King's Lynn), in Norfolk. Shortly after arriving at Bishop's Lynn his majesty was suddenly taken ill and on 12th October he decided to return to Spalding. (The name Bishop's Lynn was changed to King's Lynn by Henry VIII during his reformation of the Church.)

King John himself returned to Spalding via Wisbech but curiously chose to send his baggage train, including his Crown Jewels, by way of the causeway alongside The Wash. The King travelled safely to Swineshead Abbey, but the Crown Jewels were allegedly lost when the baggage train became trapped in the incoming tide.

Rumours abounded that this was another of King John's unscrupulous deceptions. There were accusations flying thick and fast that the King had used the jewels as security for a very large loan that he had taken out in Bishop's Lynn. Now he was claiming that unfortunately those very same jewels were tragically and irretrievably lost. Oh surely not! It would be so unlike King John to try and deceive his loyal subjects like that. We will never know the whole truth because events quickly took a different course. King John's health deteriorated rapidly and his royal court quickly moved him on to Newark-on-Trent in order to receive emergency medical help. It was to no avail. King John died at Newark Castle on October 19th 1216.

For many centuries it was thought that this unfortunate incident occurred somewhere near to Sutton Bridge on the lower River Nene. More recent use of astronomical data and computer generated tide tables for the date in question reveal that it is far more probable that this event (if it happened at all) would have been close to the present site of the Fosdyke Bridge over the River Welland. As I approach the bridge I find myself looking into the waters of the river just in case there is a glistening of gold beneath the surface. You never know your luck!

The Macmillan Way continues to follow the tidal River Welland for a further three miles until I arrive in a field just below the sluice gates that mark the lower end of the freshwater river. Shortly before reaching the sluice gates I come to the mouth of the River Glen at Surfleet Seas End.

There are two features that make the mouth of the River Glen at Surfleet Seas End such an attractive place. The first is the rather quaint boat moorings with their short wooden jetties. If you are fortunate, as I was, to visit at low tide the moored boats can be seen floating several feet below the level of their jetties, requiring the use of ladders to descend to the decks. The scene makes a rather nice photograph particularly when the sun makes the waters sparkle. Sometimes good luck smiles on me.

The second reason is to visit the excellent Ship Inn. Delicious meals and the added advantage of wooden tables on the grassy bank overlooking the moorings makes this an ideal place for either a full dining experience or a leisurely evening's drinking. I can safely pass this establishment by at the moment, but only because I have already booked in for a meal later this evening with the "Dearly Beloved".

The last part of this first section of the Macmillan Way crosses over the River Glen at the tidal sluice and passes through a chalet park. There is absolutely nobody around. This is probably because everyone will be at the annual Spalding Flower Festival which is being held today. The route then follows along the edge of Spalding Golf Club. The golf club provides the first wooded area that I have come across all day. The orange, pink, yellow and white blossoms on the trees make this a very attractive course and the greens and fairways look as though they are kept in immaculate condition.

As I emerge from the golf club driveway there is the Dearly Beloved waiting in the car ready to tell me all about her hard day at the Spalding Flower Festival.

SURFLEET TO KATES BRIDGE

DAY TWO
15 MILES

Spalding

The Macmillan Way itself skirts around the northern side of Spalding but a diversionary visit to this major town of Lincolnshire is well worthwhile.

There has been a settlement here since Roman times. The major industry during that time was the production of salt at what is today known as Wygate Park. One of the advantages this area had in those days was that it was adjacent to the sea and the final product material was therefore easy to transport. By the end of the 4th century the area was steadily silting up and as a consequence transportation of the salt became increasingly difficult.

During the 6th century the area was settled by the Anglian Spaldingas tribe from whom the current town name takes its origins. Quite incredibly, considering the combined pressures from the various rampages of the invading Vikings and Saxons, the descendants of the Spaldingas tribe were able to retain their own administration for the region until well into the 10th century. Spalding then became administered by the Kingdom of York. The Domesday Book of 1086 records the name of the town as "Spallinge".

Spalding developed as a linear settlement along the banks of the River Welland. The waterway is still a dominant feature of the town.

A little known "claim to fame" of Spalding is that it was the first place in the UK to use a bar code. On 7th October 1979 the system was introduced into Britain at the local branch of Key Markets. I wonder whatever happened to them? Well, seeing as you ask they were bought by Gateway, who were in turn bought by Somerfield who are now part of the Co-op.

The major building in Spalding is the Ayscoughfee Hall. This Grade 1 listed building was built in 1451 for the prosperous wool merchant Richard Alwyn. Ayscoughfee Hall is now used as the District Museum. There are five acres of pleasant walled gardens and a magnificent yew hedge which is believed to be one of the oldest in the country.

Before I leave Ayscoughfee Hall I must mention that it is the home of the Spalding Gentlemens Club. OK, I admit that I thought the same thing as well when I first heard about it. But this was no society with hunched men wearing grubby long macs, it was an intellectual society formed for the meeting of educated gentlemen. It was founded by Maurice Johnson in 1710 and famous former members include Sir Isaac Newton, Alexander Pope and Alfred Lord Tennyson. The collection of artefacts makes this allegedly the second oldest museum in Britain. (The oldest museum in Britain is the Ashmolean Museum, Oxford, founded in 1683. The British Museum was not founded until 1753.)

Spalding has suffered from problems with flooding for centuries. The difficulties were finally alleviated in 1953 with the opening of the Coronation Channel. This wide waterway starts at Crowland and takes water around the south of Spalding before joining the River Welland and finally emptying into The Wash.

Spalding Flower Festival

Spalding has a population of approximately 22,000 people, but that is vastly different today. I am visiting on the day of the annual Spalding Flower Festival when the numbers are swollen significantly with an influx of over 100,000 visitors.

The highlight of the Flower Festival is the Flower Parade which takes place on the first Saturday in May. Dozens of extravagantly decorated floral floats parade through Spalding. A 50 foot long float could contain up to 100,000 flower heads. You can imagine the time and effort that must be invested in the planning and decoration of the brightly coloured displays.

Back in the day Spalding was the centre of the British bulb industry. The surrounding fields were a blaze of colour in the spring, with row after row of bright tulips. Tours around the bulb fields were very popular, with people travelling vast distances just to see the extensive swathes of colours. The origins of the festival go back to the 1920's, but things really took off when the Jubilee of George V and Queen Mary coincided with the Flower Festival in 1935. It became an extravaganza and never looked back.

The first parade took place in 1959 and has become more flamboyant with each passing year. This year's theme is food. There are seemingly endless floats of giant floral cakes, fruit, vegetables, pies, chickens and virtually every other foodstuff you could care to mention. How do they make these things just from flowers? I am impressed as a giant Battenberg cake made of tulips trundles past.

The star float is known as the "Royal Float" on which the Flower Queen sits with her attendants. The Flower Queen this year (2012) is 18 years old Amy Harrisson. Next year Amy will have to crown her successor but until then her life in the local community will be one long whirl of social and civic events, from opening fetes and garden parties to attending the annual Christmas festivities.

Surfleet

The second day of the walk will be the easiest one to navigate by far. The route simply follows the River Glen upstream all the way to Kates Bridge. There will be no need for a map and compass today.

The short and easy walk to the road bridge in Surfleet makes a leisurely start to the day. However, as I approach the buildings of the village I start to wonder whether I might have overdone the ale last night. That church spire ahead definitely looks a bit wonky to me.

Fortunately it turned out that there was no need for me to be concerned, or even start to look for the nearest branch of "Specsavers". The Parish Church of St. Laurence does indeed have a leaning spire. Shortly after it was erected one side of the tower sank into the soft fenland earth and it has remained that way ever since. The tip of the spire is precisely 6ft 4½ in (1.943m) out of true perpendicular. Fenland's answer to the Leaning Tower of Pisa is best seen from the road bridge over the River Glen where the deviation appears at its most pronounced.

From Surfleet it is another couple of miles to the next village, Pinchbeck. However before then I have time for one of my little deviations to visit a place of interest.

Pinchbeck Engine House and Museum of Land Drainage

In our modern times the water is pumped from the fenlands by using electric pumps. Previously the drainage pumps were driven by diesel. During the early 19th century there was only one practical way to generate the amounts of energy required to work heavy machinery and that was to use the glorious power of steam.

I have made a diversion to view the Pinchbeck Engine which is situated just off the A16 trunk road between Boston and Spalding. Here I meet Ken Steadman who lovingly cares for the engine and the accompanying Museum of Land Drainage.

Now at first you may not think that this visit is going to take long, but I was here for over an hour. It is an absolutely fascinating place! The irrepressible Ken will personally show you everything there is to possibly know about land drainage and the engine. The climax comes when he fires up the giant beam engine and the wheels turn, the pistons pump and the water wheel duly turns again.

In the 1630's Sir Philibert Vernatti started to drain Deeping Fen by cutting Vernatt's Drain through Pinchbeck to the River Welland just downstream of Spalding. Initially all went according to plan and the land started to drain. Then the unexpected happened. Until that time what the engineers did not know about land drainage was that as the fenland drained it also shrank. Then they discovered that when it shrank it shrank lots! What is more (or less according to your viewpoint) it kept on shrinking. Soon the land was below the level of the drains so windmills had to be used to lift the water to the rivers. As the ground continued to sink so the water had to be lifted higher and higher until the point was reached where either a reduction in wind or increase in water caused the fens to flood again.

The arrival of steam power literally turned the tide, and the fens could be drained efficiently once again. The first steam engine was installed at Pode Hole in 1826 with the engine at Pinchbeck being constructed seven years later.

The Pinchbeck Engine was made in 1833 by the Butterley Company in Leeds. For the technically minded it is a rotative beam engine mounted on an A-frame. The single cylinder has a 35 inch (89cm) bore and when it was working at its peak generated a maximum of 20 horsepower (15kW). The engine powered a 22ft (6.71m) diameter wheel fitted with 40 paddles. This device could lift 7,600 gallons (34,000L) of water every minute through a height of 8 feet. During the course of a year the engine would pump around 3,000,000 gallons of water away from the surrounding land. In a typical year the steam driven pump would be working for approximately 180 days, consuming coal at the rate of 1cwt (50.8kg) every hour.

The Pinchbeck Engine was replaced with an electric pumping station is 1952 and the old steam engine became obsolete. Engineering enthusiasts restored the steam engine and it was opened to the public in 1979. Unfortunately the steam boiler was unable to be restored into a safe working mode so electricity has to be used for demonstration purposes.

The Pinchbeck Engine provides a reminder that without the availability of steam technology to pump away the surplus water the fens would have been a very different (and very watery) place.

The engine house and museum is currently only open for visitors on Monday, Wednesday and Friday. It is well worth a visit and Ken will be delighted to show you around.

Pinchbeck Fen Slipe

Returning to the MacMillan Way by the side of the River Glen there is a very distant glimpse of some low hills over to my right. It just emphasises to me that the fenlands are very, very flat. I would not think that the members of the Spalding Mountain Rescue Team have many call-outs.

Pinchbeck Fen Slipe is a narrow strip of Nature Reserve extending for some 2 ½ miles alongside the River Glen. The unusual name derives from Slipe Drove, a road running parallel to the river only a short distance away from the Reserve. When the river runs high the waters flood the grassland to the side, creating pools and wetlands. In turn this leads to the establishment of areas of water crowfoot, patches of water violet and yellow loosestrife. Yellow rattle, common fleabane and ragged robin can also be found here.

There is also a prolific population of birds. Crested Grebe, Mallard, Reed Warbler, Reed Bunting and Whitethroat all regularly make their nests here. According to the locals there are also Barn Owls which can sometimes be seen if one is fortunate enough.

It is the Barn Owl that prompted the Hawk and Owl Trust to erect several large nesting boxes along the bank of the River Glen. There are two at Pinchbeck Slipe and I will be passing several others before I reach Kates Bridge. They are easily seen atop their high support poles. The boxes are intended to keep their occupants safe from predators. Unfortunately, as is sometimes the case with these well intentioned ideas, nature does not always behave in the most obliging manner. Whilst the occasional Barn Owl may have initially made use of their new purpose-built dwellings, flocks of aggressive jackdaw squatters found them even more to their liking and have firmly established themselves as the prime residents.

The fens have their own flat-look beauty, but sadly in the distance over to my left I have noticed eight of the greatest eyesores of our time sticking obtrusively up into what should be a perfect sky. In the middle of this table-top landscape someone has seen fit to erect eight ugly steel windmills. No doubt some will say that these are essential for the future of our planet but nobody has yet convinced me that they are anything but an economic nonsense and a very nasty blot on the landscape. If they are so essential then why are only two out of the eight of them actually turning?

Guthram, King of the Danelaw

On the opposite bank at the end of Pinchbeck Nature Reserve is Guthram Gowt, which is a sluice that derives its name after

Guthram, the Danish King of the Danelaw. The Danelaw was the name given to the Danish occupied lands of England towards the end of the Dark Ages.

From about 786 AD the Danish began a series of raids to the north east parts of the English coast. As the years passed by the raids became more frequent and at some point the raiders decided it would be easier to bring their families over here with them rather than keep commuting across the North Sea to indulge in their looting and pillaging. The Danish gradually transformed from raiders into immigrants and started to develop regular settlements. Gradually the Danes were able to establish a strong ruling presence, taking control of the Kingdom of York and extending their influence towards East Anglia.

Inevitably there were struggles and conflicts between different groups of Danes. By 874 King Guthram had consolidated his authority over the Danish occupied lands and began to turn his attention to expanding his rule into Mercia and Northumberland. Two years later in 876 Guthram had established a position where he could reach out for the great prize, the West Saxon Kingdom of Wessex. The only person who stood in his way was the much celebrated and popular King Alfred.

The Danes sailed to the South Coast near to Poole Harbour and attacked the Saxon forces. Guthram quickly gained the upper hand but Alfred managed to negotiate a temporary peace settlement. The next year this was broken by Guthram who led his invading army deeper into Wessex, capturing the town of Exeter in the process. At Chippenham on 6th January 878 Guthram sprung a surprise night time attack on King Alfred's army and the Saxon King was forced to flee.

Alfred rebuilt his forces and on 12th May 878 confronted the Danes at Ethandun, which is believed to be at the place now known as Edington, Wiltshire. This time the men of Wessex were victorious and Alfred laid down the treaty terms for the surrender of the Danes.

The agreement became known as the Treaty of Wedmore. King Guthram and the Danes were ordered to immediately leave Wessex and in future they were to be restricted to stay within the boundaries of East Anglia and East Mercia. In addition Alfred demanded that Guthram convert to the Christian faith, forcing him to be baptised and to recognise King Alfred as his Godfather. From this point in time Guthram adopted the Christian name of Aethelstan.

Guthram (now called Aethelstan) lived out the rest of his life in East Anglia. He died in 890 and is believed to be buried at Hadleigh in Suffolk.

Remember Guthrum and his nemesis, King Alfred. We will be meeting up with them again after another 210 miles.

Baston Fen

Baston Fen is a long and narrow stretch of pasture of approximately one mile in length. During the winter the pastures will always flood, making Baston the ideal home for numerous species of wildfowl. It is not uncommon to see thousands of birds here at peak times. There are also many clumps of willow and alder that provide shelter for finches, tits and warblers.

The top of the bank is extremely muddy along this section. The rich grasses are grazed by a large herd of cows which wander from end to end churning up the path as they go. Recent rains have turned this embankment into a real quagmire and it is sometimes much easier, if slightly more precarious, to walk along the steep sides of the bank.

Kates Bridge

For two days now I have been walking across the fens. I have mentioned before how flat everything is out here. The landscape has been very strange to a person like me who lives on the edge of the Cotswolds. Over the last few miles the westward horizon has gradually developed some shape and now as I cover the last few fields towards Kates Bridge the fuzzy grey silhouettes are beginning to take on some colour as well. I can see some hills!

Another recent development that I have become aware of is that while passing through the last few fields the raised embankments on either side of the River Glen have gradually become relatively lower. Crossing the last field the bank finally merges into the general land and the ridge that I have been following all of the way from Surfleet Seas End has gone.

You might at first expect that Kates Bridge takes its name from a former fair maiden of these parts and that a racy story is about to unfold. Unfortunately no such luck. We are back to the Danes once again. There has been a bridge at this location since early times and the name allegedly takes its origin from a Danish god, known as Kat or Catta depending on scholastic interpretation.

There is very good reason for a bridge to be sited here. This point is the lowest place along the River Glen where there is a stone river bed, making this the only crossing point where early man could ford the river. It was an obvious location for our ancestors to build a bridge. Kates Bridge itself no longer provides the crossing for the main thoroughfare. That is the task of a much newer structure that now carries the A15.

At one time Kate's Bridge was also the limit of the navigable sections of the River Glen. Corn and wool were transported from Kates Bridge downstream to Boston. The development of the railways caused this route to become uneconomic and the top end gradually fell into disrepair. The practical navigable river now has its upstream limit at Bourne Eau pumping station some three miles downstream from Kates Bridge.

Kates Bridge forms a distinct end to the fenland section of the Macmillan Way. I have travelled thirty miles across the flat landscape but now there is a slope ahead of me. The flat and largely featureless landscape has meant that I have been exposed to the elements but I have also enjoyed the wildness of it all. From here on the geology becomes one of constant Jurassic Limestone all of the way to Abbotsbury.

The Dorset coast is still some 260 miles distant.

KATES BRIDGE TO EASTON ON THE HILL

DAY 3

11 MILES

Onwards to Rutland

I start today with something I have not yet experienced on this adventure; a walk uphill. Admittedly this is only a short incline but it is still a slope nonetheless. There are also some stones visible in the fields. A further reminder that now I am passing through a very different terrain.

The first two hours are spent merrily following the Macmillan Way along a mixture of field paths and narrow lanes. I am taken through as a series of small villages, Obthorpe, Wilsthorpe, Braceborough and Greatford. It is a very pleasant and leisurely start to the day.

One of my little quirks when I am out on my walks is to take note of the dedications of the churches. The vast majority of the time they have common dedications such as All Saints, St. Peter or St. Michael. Much rarer but far more interesting to me are the churches which are dedicated to the Saints that I have never heard of before. This causes me to delve into the reference library with great enthusiasm.

Wilsthorpe Church is such a case in point. The building is Grade II listed and was completed in 1715. The front entrance possesses an attractive and unusual arched doorway. It is the dedication to St. Faith that aroused my curiosity. Who was St. Faith?

I had initially anticipated that I was going to be led down the road of the virtues of Faith, Hope and Charity but I was a long way off the mark. St. Faith is also known by her French name of Sainte Foy. She was born in Agen, Aquitaine during the mid 3rd century. Sometime around 290AD Foy fell foul of the Roman authorities who had ordered the people to make pagan sacrifices. Faith refused to comply and as punishment for her defiance was put to death by torture with hot irons. The Church elevated Faith to be made a Saint in recognition of her dedication to her Christian beliefs. St. Faith became adopted as the patron of pilgrims, prisoners and soldiers. Her Feast Day is celebrated on October 6th.

Greatford

Greatford is a pleasant village and there are some sizeable houses here. Greatford Hall was built by Elizabeth I in the 16th century but it is a later owner, Doctor Francis Willis, who provides the most interest.

Francis Willis was born on August 17th 1718. He studied at Brasenose College, Oxford and was initially ordained as a priest. Following his marriage Willis pursued a medical career and after qualifying in medicine served as a physician in Lincoln. At Lincoln he began to develop an interest in the mentally disturbed and began to build a reputation as a specialist for successful psychiatric treatments.

In 1776 Francis moved to Greatford Hall where he started to treat patients at his own home, gradually turning it into his private sanatorium. Willis strongly believed that many disorders could be treated with exposure to fresh air and vigorous activity. The country environment allowed him to develop his work along these themes. It was nothing unusual to see the labourers in the fields around Greatford smartly dressed in black coats and wearing powdered wigs. Closer inspection would reveal that they were all wealthy gentlemen undergoing treatment from Dr. Willis.

It was in 1788 that Dr. Willis was presented with his best known patient, none other than King George III. The King suffered from repeated bouts of madness, which was probably the disorder now recognised as porphyria. An equerry recommended Dr. Willis to the Queen after Willis had successfully treated the equerry's mother-in-law from similar symptoms.

The good doctor treated the King just as he would have done any other patient. His trademark blend of kindness and consideration combined with hard manual labour on the farmland released George III from his torment. King George was so grateful to Francis Willis that he rewarded him with £1000 a year for the next 21 years. Francis son

Dr John Wills, who also assisted with the treatment, was awarded £650 per year.

Following the successful treatment of the King word of Dr.Willis quickly spread through Georgian society and the demand for his services soared. The increase in patient numbers resulted in Willis establishing a second private asylum at nearby Shillingthorpe Hall.

The King suffered a relapse in 1801 and returned to Shillingthorpe for more treatment. This time the younger son, Robert Willis, also helped to rehabilitate the King. Unfortunately George III suffered a further downturn in 1810. This time he was not so fortunate and all of the efforts of the Willis family could not prevent the illness taking a fatal toll.

The story of the King's illness is told in the award winning film "The Madness of King George" released in 1994. In the film the role of Dr. Willis is played by Ian Holm. King George III was memorably played by Nigel Hawthorne for which performance he received a BAFTA "Best Actor" award.

There is a memorial bust to Dr. Francis Willis in the Greatford Church of Thomas Beckett. This memorial was created by the celebrated English sculptor Joseph Nollekins (1737 – 1823).

Greatford Hall suffered from extensive fire damage in 1922. The Hall was afterwards completely rebuilt in the same style. Unfortunately Greatford Hall is not open to visits by the general public. At least it is still standing which is more than can be said for Shillingthorpe Hall. That was demolished in 1949 and nothing now remains of the former sanatorium.

The Macmillan Way takes me across the former Shillingthorpe Park. There are no well dressed Georgian gentlemen to be seen at work in the fields today.

It is in this former parkland that I cross a small footbridge and say a final fond farewell to the River Glen. The waters are now but a small stream known as the West Glen. It has served me well all the way from Surfleet Seas End and now I must move on.

Bridleways

A further sign that I am moving on is the notice that tells me that I am now entering Rutland, England's smallest county.

Soon after crossing the county line I turn into Seven Acre Wood and have my first encounter with a type of right of way that will become one of the banes of my life during this expedition. I am about to do battle with my first official Bridle Way.

The image often conjured up by the term "bridle way" is one of a wide, grassy track that is easy to walk along. True, there are some like that particularly on open countryside. However when it comes to woodland things can turn out to be very different. The horse's hooves can rapidly churn up the ground into mud. Then the tree cover does not allow this area to dry properly, and with more rain and more horses the mud gradually becomes deeply pitted by their hooves and eventually becomes totally waterlogged. The riders of the next horses through will avoid the worst of the gunge by keeping to the dryer sides of the track, so increasing the muddy area until it fills the full width. Hence for a bridle way the walker should read very wet and muddy. Where the guidebook states "muddy bridle way" be prepared to become stuck up to your knees for days on end or at the very least lose your wellies. If it is suggested that conditions will be both wet and muddy you would probably be advised to take your own canoe!

You have probably gathered from the above rant this path proved to be hard going. It was a very muddy and exhausted hiker who finally emerged at the other end of the bridle way at Cobbs Nook Farm.

The gateway to Cobbs Nook Farm also marks the highest point of the walk so far. From the flat fenlands sitting scarcely above sea level I had now risen to the dizzy height of one hundred and fifty feet.

Below me lays the elegant Georgian town of Stamford and I make my way down the gentle slope towards its welcoming stone buildings.

Stamford

Stamford is a delightful town with a population of approximately 22,000 people. It was the first "Conservation Town" in Britain, being designated with this classification in 1967. The town has been able to maintain a high standard of architectural importance and boasts over 600 protected buildings which is a very impressive number. The majority of the buildings are constructed from the local Jurassic limestone, giving a distinctive Georgian feel to the town. Stamford also gains an extra dimension because dotted among the stone structures are some fine examples of older timber-framed buildings. Much of the street layout has not changed noticeably since Saxon times, which has left picturesque open squares and quaint narrow alleyways.

Stamford owes its primary importance as do so many similar cases around Britain to its strategic location. Situated on the banks of the River Welland it was the main crossing point for early travellers from London to the north. The Romans built Ermine Street, their main road to York and onwards to Hadrians Wall, through here. At that time the ford was situated between the two Roman military encampments of Castor to the south and Greater Casterton to the north. Castor is the Latin word for camp.

Stamford developed under the rule of the Saxons who bequeathed the name "Stony Ford" from which the present name is derived. The Danish invasions of the 9th century did not do Stamford any favours with constant strife by different factions to secure ownership of the crossing. Once the town was back in Saxon hands it began to prosper again. So important did Stamford become to the Saxons that in 972 King Edgar bestowed it with borough status. Edgar also granted Stamford the right to have its own mint to produce coins. The Saxons increased the defensive properties of Stamford by building a fort on the banks of the River Welland.

The river crossing also became of great strategic importance to the Norman conquerors. The invaders needed to protect both their key route to Scotland and also to control the quickly growing town. In 1075 they built a much larger castle on the original Saxon site in order to protect their interests.

Stamford became renowned during medieval times for its pottery. From the 9th century to the 13th century the town produced the majority of the glazed pottery in England. The area was also noted for the quality of its wool, with "Stamford cloth" being highly regarded throughout Europe.

It was, however, always the road that was to give Stamford its exalted position with the ruling powers. Edward I, Henry VIII, Elizabeth I and Mary Queen of Scots were all frequent visitors. Charles I visited the town once and then promptly wished he hadn't. He was betrayed to the Roundhead forces whilst staying at Stamford resulting in his capture the very next day. He was eventually tried and then executed for high treason.

The current road through Stamford is the A1, formerly known as the Great North Road, which connects London and Edinburgh.

The preservation of the architecture of Stamford probably gained an advantage from the late arrival of the railway to the town. This enabled the borough to avoid all of the worst excesses of the industrial revolution and helped to retain the majority of its original Georgian buildings.

Stamford is one of the Eleanor Cross locations. When Edward I's wife, Eleanor of Castille died at Lincoln in 1290, her body was transferred for burial to Westminster Abbey. The long journey required twelve overnight stops and following the funeral Edward I ordered twelve crosses to be erected at each of the sites where his wife's body had rested overnight. Initially these were just simple wooden crosses, but were gradually replaced with ornate stone monuments. The original crosses were situated at Lincoln, Grantham, Stamford, Geddington, Hardingstone, Stony Stratford, Woburn, Dunstable, St.Albans, Waltham, Westcheap and Charing. Of the twelve crosses the only three that remain today can be seen at Geddington,

Hardingstone and Waltham. Stamford has a modern representation of an "Eleanor Cross". A tall stone needle stands outside the "Golden Fleece" pub.

Stamford was formerly a great ecclesiastical centre. When the Royal Charter was granted by Henry III in 1256 Stamford boasted six monasteries, six religious colleges and no less than fourteen churches. Such was the educational standing of Stamford that in 1333 a group of rebellious Oxford students originating from Merton and Brasenose Colleges, Oxford, attempted to form their own breakaway university in the town. The authorities did not share their enthusiasm for a new home and King Edward III ordered the students to return to Oxford. A whole local industry grew up around the monasteries and churches, which gave employment to many local people. The Dissolution of the Monasteries by Henry VIII in 1539 caused a severe decline in the local economy.

The High Street is pedestrianised but it has a very different look to many similar sized towns. Whereas many town centres all look the same with the national retail chains all displaying their standard branded shop fronts, Stamford has successfully kept its individual appearance. The retail giants have been made to conform to the local architecture and there are a wide variety of individual shop fronts. This variety is further enhanced with a large number of independent retailers mixed among the more familiar names.

One thing I am not prepared for is the former church of St. Michael's in the High Street. There has been a church on this site since 1158. During extensive repairs in 1832 the whole structure collapsed causing the church to be completely rebuilt. Migration of people away from the town centre to the outlying parts of the town meant that the church became surplus to requirements during the middle of the last century. An innovative person suggested turning it into a row of shops and that is what happened in 1970. The top of the building still has the appearance of a church, but the ground floor shops are of a smart modern design. They certainly look as though they blend in well with the rest of the town. I can't help thinking that the marketing people at M&S missed out by not having a shop here. They could have been selling St.Michael at St.Micheal's.

After walking the length of the High Street I turn down a narrow alley, pass the old castle walls and come out onto an open area by the River Welland known as The Meadows. They were previously known as "Bull Meadows" and it was on this grassy area that the annual bull running festival was held. The festival took place every year from the early 13th century until the middle of the 19th century.

The story is that during the reign of King John (see, he crops up yet again), William de Warenne, 5th Earl of Surrey was placed in charge of Stamford Castle. One day he was looking out from his battlements when he saw two bulls fighting on this field. Two butchers were sent out to quell the beasts, but one of the bulls raced off and charged into the town. De Warenne reacted by mounting his horse and chasing the bull through the streets of Stamford until he succeeded in forcing it back out to the meadow. He enjoyed himself so much that he granted the ownership of the meadows to the town in perpetuity provided that on each November 13th the townspeople supplied a bull to be set loose in the streets so that it could be chased out into the meadow. The bull was then captured and slaughtered with the townspeople feasting on the meat. This practise continued every year until 1839 when campaigns were mounted by the Society for the Protection of Animals which resulted in the banning of the festival.

The path across The Meadows passes by a an information board that tells me that in AD61 the raddled remnants of the IX Legion fled over the ford here hotly pursued by Queen Boudicca and her Iceni army.

It is with some sadness that I depart from Stamford. It is a very attractive stone town and really justifies me allocating more time to enjoy its splendours. I thoroughly recommend it to you for a day out, but meanwhile I have to make my way to Easton on the Hill or I will not complete this stage in the planned time.

Easton on the Hill

From Stamford the Macmillan Way joins with the Hereward Way to take me all the way to the Rutland county town of Oakham.

This long-distance footpath links Harling, Norfolk with Oakham and is dedicated to the memory of the Saxon rebel Hereward the Wake who was a scourge of William the Conqueror and the Norman invaders. Hereward established his outlaw headquarters at the cathedral city of Ely, which is located near the middle of the route. The path leads me out of Stamford and follows the River Welland upstream for a short way before crossing over the water at Broadeng Bridge.

The hill up to Easton is the hardest climb of the walk so far. In the greater scope of things it is as nothing compared to the later sharp breathless inclines of the Cotswolds, but after two days of fenland walking it is still a shock to the system. It does not help that it is extremely wet on the slopes and it was sometimes a case of two steps forward and one slide back.

Easton is a very attractive village of delightful stone houses and cottages. The village is recorded in the Domesday Book as "Estone".

The small "Priest's House" is one of the smallest buildings owned by the National Trust, and is open to the public on a limited number of days or by appointment. The original building dates from the 16th century, but was transformed by extensive restoration work in 1867.

The main industry around Easton used to be the Collyweston Slate industry. During the latter parts of the 19th century and early 20th century around 200 people were employed locally to quarry and produce the ironstone slate. Production then declined and finally came to an end during the 1950's. A small exhibition of the history of Collyweston slate can be seen at The Priest's House.

EASTON ON THE HILL TO OAKHAM

DAY 4

14 MILES

Ketton

Ketton is the fourth largest settlement in the county of Rutland. Illustrating just how small Rutland is in comparison to other English counties Ketton achieves this lofty status with a population of just under 1,700 people.

The village is identified as "Chetene" in the Domesday Book, which means "banks of the Chater", deriving its name from the river that flows through the village. Ketton as I find it today is really an amalgamation of three smaller villages, Ketton, Aldgate and Geeston, which have gradually merged together over the centuries.

Ketton's most noted resident was Robert of Ketton, who was born here circa. 1110 AD. Robert became a learned scholar and with his fellow student and friend Herman of Carinthia set off in 1134 to travel through the Byzantium Empire and the Crusades areas of Palestine. Both men became expert Arabic translators and eventually settled in Spain which at that time had become a base for Arabic scholars.

Robert met with "Peter the Venerable" a French Abbot who wished to have access to Arabic religious texts but was unable to read the language for himself. This set Robert on the path towards his great work, the translation of the Koran into Latin. He completed his masterpiece in 1143 and it became the standard reference work for European scholars until well into the 16th century.

There is a lovely three-arched stone bridge that takes me over the small River Chater. This is followed by an elevated walkway past the impressive church of St.Mary's with its tall spire and elegant stone arches.

Ketton Quarry

The guidebook warns me of a large quarry. The signposts warn me of a large quarry. The Ordnance Survey map clearly shows a large quarry. So I am prepared for a large quarry. What I am not prepared for is the ground opening up into a giant chasm in which you could easily lose a whole town! This big hole currently occupies 68 acres (27.5 hectares) and is still expanding.

The sheer scale of the workings is overwhelming. Dumper trucks with enormous wheels are running backwards and forwards ferrying the stone to the main buildings, while large diggers refill them again from the heaps of quarried material.

The quarry produces oolitic limestone that is used both for stone building blocks and for the production of cement. Ketton cement works started manufacturing in 1928 and produces nearly 10% of the total UK demand for Portland cement. The current owners of the business are Heidelberg Cement.

A small consolation for this noisy and dusty intrusion into the countryside is that the owners have provided a bridge across the quarry so that I do not have to walk around this yawning hole. From the almost pristine appearance of the bridge this facility must be a relatively new innovation. The guidebook does not mention a bridge and even the latest internet updates that I have downloaded of the route advised that I should be prepared for long diversions. It is a welcome change to be provided with an unexpected short cut! Crossing the bridge provides me with excellent views of the quarry sides. The different limestone strata are clearly visible with their subtle changes of colour tone.

As is often the case these days some of the disused areas around the quarry have been given over to become a nature reserve. The Ketton Quarry Reserve is managed by the Leicester and Rutland Wildlife Trust and has been designated a Site of Special Scientific Interest (SSSI). Bee Orchids, Cowslip, Vipers Burgloss, and Carline Thistle thrive on the limestone soils. There is a relatively rare plant that grows here, the Yellow Birds Nest, sometimes referred to as Dutchman's Pipe. This fleshy plant grows up to 1ft (30cm) tall and contains absolutely no chlorophyll at all. This gives the entire plant a light yellow colouring. The plant obtains its nourishment from fungi and leaf mould. Another novelty with this plant is that it produces two differently coloured flowers. The spring flower is yellow, but the later flower that appears in the autumn is a light red.

Interesting though they are it may not be too clever of me to go poking about among the plants because this area is also a favoured haunt of Britain's only poisonous snake, the adder.

Butterflies also thrive here. The cool and damp conditions today are not conducive to these delicate creatures but on a brighter and calmer day I would be able to see the Marbled White and Dingy Skipper among other varieties.

Left to her own devices Mother Nature would soon cover the entire wild area with scrub. The Wildlife Trust has countered this by introducing a flock of Manx Loughton pedigree sheep to graze upon it. Grazing will keep down the scrub and enable an area of limestone grassland to develop.

Rutland

As they say, "Size isn't everything"

Biggest is not always the best and the county of Rutland positively revels in its minimalistic delights. The county motto "Multum in Parvo" meaning "Much in Little" was officially adopted by the council in 1950 to boast of the many joys that can be found here.

Rutland is the smallest English county. There have been several attempts over the years to absorb it into one of the surrounding counties but each time little Rutland just bounces back to reclaim its own independent status.

The county extends for 18 miles (29 km) north to south and 17 miles (27.4km) east to west. Those distances are measured at its widest points. The total area is a mere 147 square miles with only the City of London having a smaller coverage. The population of 37,400

(2011 census) puts it firmly at the bottom of any table of the unitary authorities of the United Kingdom. If it was reclassified as a district then it would still be in the "relegation zone" rising to 348th out of 354 official UK Districts.

Rutland only boasts two towns, the county town of Oakham and the smaller Uppingham. Everything else is made up of villages and hamlets. The majority of the buildings in Rutland are constructed from the local limestone with either Collyweston stone slates or reed thatched roofs.

Our good friend King John turns up yet again. When John married his second wife, Isabella of Angueleme (1188 – 1246), Rutland was assigned as the wedding dowry.

The terrain mainly features low hills interspersed with fertile river valleys. The biggest single geographical feature is Rutland Water which will be covered in the next section.

All of the rural fresh air and open countryside of Rutland must have its benefits. Two interesting facts emerged from my researches. Firstly Rutland is officially the happiest county in the United Kingdom. A survey carried out during 2012 placed this small area firmly at the top of the smiley table. The second fact is that Rutland has the highest fertility rate in the UK with the average woman giving birth to 2.81 children. I will leave you to ponder over whether there is any direct connection between these two pieces of information.

Rutland Water

Rutland Water is one of the largest man-made reservoirs in Europe covering an area of 4.19 square miles (10.86 sq.km.). The reservoir holds approximately 124,000 cubic metres of water. In total area it is only slightly smaller than Windermere which is England's largest lake.

The massive dam at the east end of the reservoir is 115ft high (35m) high, extends for 1,300 yards (1,200m) in length and is a chunky 890 yards (810m) thick at the base. It was constructed from the clay dug out from the reservoir site. The dam was completed in 1975 and the reservoir was filled during 1976.

Rutland Water sits in the valley of the small River Gwash. The Gwash flows into the reservoir at Oakham, out again at the dam end, and then continues its passage to discharge into the River Welland. Water for the reservoir is pumped into it by pipelines from the River Welland and River Nene.

A very distinguishing feature is a peninsula that protrudes into the reservoir from the north west corner. This finger of land holds the small village of Upper Hambledon which was high enough to avoid it being submerged when the valley was flooded. Its neighbouring villages of Nether Hambledon and Middle Hambledon were not so fortunate and lie somewhere out there beneath the surface of the water.

Possibly the most famous landmark on Rutland Water is to be found on the south shore. St. Matthews Church at Normanton has been preserved in a unique fashion. The church was deconsecrated in 1970 and was originally planned for demolition. There was such an outcry from the general public that a compromise was agreed. The lower part of the church was filled with rubble and a concrete cap was sealed over it. When the valley was flooded the church remained on the bank, with the lower part of the nave sunk into the ground, leaving the tower and upper part of the nave and roof still visible. The former church is now used as a local museum.

Rutland Water is a bird watchers paradise. There are over 20,000 wildfowl living on the water and in its margins. The East side of the reservoir is specifically dedicated as a nature reserve with shallow lagoons providing an ideal habitat for the birds. There are two centres for bird watching here, the main visitor centre at Lyndon and a smaller area at Egleton. There are 31 bird watching hides that enable visitors to remain concealed and not cause disturbances that will frighten the birds away.

Where do I start with the variety of birds that can be seen here? Lapwing, Coot, Shoveler, Gadwall, Goldeneye, Pochard, Tufted Duck, Teal, Swan, Wigeon, Cormorant and Grebe provide the majority of the population, but there is one bird above all others that I will be keeping a lookout for as I walk around the edge of the north shore; the magnificent Osprey.

Ospreys were introduced to Rutland water in 1996 and there are now regular breeding pairs that return to the reservoir each year to raise their chicks.

The Osprey has a 5ft (150cm) wingspan. The upper plumage is brown with a cream under part. The cock has a distinctive "highwayman's mask" across its eyes while the slightly heavier hen has a significant breast band.

The real cachet would be to observe an osprey seize its prey. The bird will dive towards the water with its wings held back, targeting the fish that are swimming just under the surface. At the very last moment the osprey will shoot its talons forward and grab hold of the fish and take it away for consumption. About one dive in four will successfully produce a meal for the mature osprey. Less experienced younger birds usually require several more attempts to obtain their dinner.

The osprey builds a large nest of up to one metre wide and prefers high isolated locations within three to four kilometres of a major piece of water. A flat-topped tree would suit them very well and be a "des res" for the aspiring osprey family.

The female lays two or three eggs in late April. They are about the size of a hen's egg and are a blotchy reddish-brown colour. After hatching the fledglings will stay around the nest for seven or eight weeks before leaving it for the first time. They will often return to scrounge a meal from their parents should their attempts at fending for themselves prove to be a struggle. A scenario well known to us humans when our own children come back home from university! (Except that the osprey does not bring a bag of washing with them).

The osprey departs for sunnier climes in late August, preferring to take their holidays in West Africa or the southern part of the Iberian Peninsula. They will start to return to Rutland in March.

Younger birds may not return for two to five years, but eventually they will feel that the time is right to return to their place of birth and start the whole cycle over again.

The path is a real delight as it gently twists its way around the north shore, taking me in and out of the inlets and promontories of Rutland Water. Birds, insects, squirrels and rabbits could be seen going about their daily activities. A few yacht sails were visible out on the water, and there were many boats occupied by anglers all trying to tempt the resident trout into mistaking their flies for the genuine article.

It is easy walking and I was able to proceed at a steady pace along the well-kept path. This means that I will be well up with my schedule for the day and I will make Oakham in good time. Having plenty of time in reserve enabled me to take advantage of the many seats spread along the path for the benefit of walkers and I spent some time sitting on a selection of them while contemplating the scenery. Sometimes it is nice to just sit a while and drink in the surroundings.

Oakham

Oakham has a population of just 10,000 according to the latest 2011 census. That makes Oakham the largest town in the smallest county. Is that the equivalent of being the tallest dwarf? Seeing as you ask, the tallest Disney dwarf was Bashful. This does not fit with either Oakham or Rutland. They are both more like the smallest dwarf which was Happy. Is there something subliminal here? Both the smallest county and the smallest dwarf are Happy.

Oakham is quite a lovely little place and there is plenty for the visitor to see. Much to my own quirky delight there are some quite interesting snippets of trivia to delve into.

Oakham Castle was built between 1180 and 1190 for Walchelin de Ferrers, Lord of the Manor of Oakham. It is not really a castle as we would first think of it, more of a fortified manor house. All that remains now is the Great Hall, which is recognised as one of the finest examples of domestic Norman architecture. It is open to visitors.

The east wall of the hall is home to a collection of large decorated horseshoes. This unusual assembly originates from the traditional custom that every royal person who visited Oakham should forfeit a horseshoe to the Lord of the Manor. The inverted horseshoe was the symbol of the de Ferrers family since Henry de Ferrer arrived in England with William the Conqueror. Ferrer is the French equivalent of the word farrier. The same symbol is found in the Rutland coat of arms and is also used as the emblem for Ruddles ale.

There are now 230 horseshoes on the wall. The earliest recorded donation was a plain horse shoe given by Edward IV in 1470. The most recent was from Princess Alexandra in 2005. Horse shoes are traditionally hung with the gape at the top, allegedly to catch all of the good luck. Inverted horse shoes are reputed to be unlucky, permitting all of the luck to be poured away. The argument in favour of having an inverted horse shoe is that it is exhibited that way to stop the devil from sitting in the bowl. It sounds as though with horse shoes you just can't win!

Near to the castle is the Butter Cross. I will see a few more of these structures during my excursion, but this one is a well maintained example of these old-style market houses. The Buttercross at Oakham is octagonal in shape with a pyramid roof.

The very mention of Oakham sent me back to my childhood. To a young boy during the 1960's the name Oakham had a mystical significance. It was the name on the signal box that had a pride of place on his model railway layout. Hornby and Airfix both used the design of the Oakham signal box for their scale models. So you can understand that I simply had to take a slight deviation from the designated Macmillan Way in order to see the real thing for the very first time.

This signal box is instantly recognisable to anyone who ever had a model train set. It was first constructed in 1899 and is now officially classified as a listed building.

Unlike some railway features you do not have to risk life and limb to see it. The signal box stands right next to the road and it was like seeing a long-lost friend as soon as I turned the street corner. There it was, carefully preserved and just as I remembered it from all of those years ago. Same shape, same colours and the same simple nameplate, "Oakham".

Jeffrey Hudson

In all of the good cowboy films someone always seemed to say "This town ain't big enough for both of us". That could never have been said of Jeffrey Hudson because he was the small man from the small county. Hudson was born in Oakham in 1619 and when he was seven years old he had reached all of eighteen inches (45cm) in height. He was still the same height when he reached thirty.

Jeffrey Hudson first came to prominence when on his seventh birthday he was taken into the household of Lord Buckingham and his wife. Jeffrey's father was the keeper of Lord Buckingham's baiting bulls. Lord and Lady Buckingham were much taken with the little fellow.

A few months after Jeffrey had joined the household the Buckingham's were entertaining King Charles I and his wife Queen Henrietta Maria. The final course of the dinner was a huge pie that was brought to the dining room uncut. When the pie was put before the Royals young Jeffrey burst through the crust dressed in a miniature suit of armour. The Queen was delighted and immediately took young Hudson into her court bestowing him with the title of the Queen's Dwarf.

Incredible as it may seem Hudson fought an active part in the Civil War. As you may have expected from his upbringing he was firmly on the Royalist side. When the Queen was forced to flee to France in 1643 Hudson was one of the trusted courtiers sent to accompany her. By this time Hudson was tiring of being the constant butt of jokes and made it crystal clear that he was not going to put up with it any more. Inevitably someone else made a joke about his diminutive size and an outraged Hudson challenged the offender to a duel. The outcome was that Hudson shot his opponent through the head, killing him instantly.

At that time duelling had been declared illegal in France and Hudson's punishment was to be expelled from the court. (So it was not that illegal to punish him with imprisonment, or even worse).

The next part of the story becomes somewhat blurred, but it transpires that somehow Hudson was captured by Barbary Pirates and taken to North Africa as a slave. He remained in Algeria or Tunisia for twenty five years until he managed to devise a way of returning to England in 1669. Hudson's period of captivity had an amazing side benefit. He experienced a growth spurt. Jeffrey was now all of 39 inches tall!

Jeffrey Hudson returned to Oakham for a few years where he lived with his brother. In 1676 he left the town to go to London, probably with the intention to ingratiate himself back into the Royal Court now that the monarchy had been restored. It would be fair to say that his return to London could have gone better. The return coincided with a turbulent political period and Hudson managed to get himself entangled in the "Popish Plot" with Titus Oates. It may have been more than simple coincidence that Titus Oates also originally hailed from Oakham, although he was 30 years younger than Hudson. Jeffrey's involvement in this affair caused him to be imprisoned at the Gatehouse prison until 1680 when he was released.

Nothing is known about the remainder of Jeffrey Hudson's life. He was reported as being dead in 1682, but nobody knows how or where this happened.

It is an extraordinary life story for the man once known to royal courtiers as Lord Minimus. A man of whom King Charles I was alleged to have said "The Rutland motto Multum in Parvo applies just as aptly to our little Jeffrey".

OAKHAM TO BRAMPTON ASH

DAY 5

17 MILES

Brooke, Belton-in-Rutland, Allexton

I have reached another change in the terrain. After leaving Oakham the Macmillan Way follows a south westerly course, cutting a line though the remainder of Rutland, a corner of Leicestershire and a long trail through Northamptonshire to the edge of the Cotswolds.

Much of my route for the next five days will be composed of a succession of farm fields interspersed with stone-built small villages.

I pass through Brooke where a small stone bridge takes me over the tiny infant River Gwash. Looking down on the stream it is difficult to picture that this is the same water course that is dammed only a few miles further on to create the vast expanse of Rutland Water.

Priors Coppice Nature Reserve covers 29 hectares and is a relic from days long past. Much of the woodland was cleared by our ancestors for their settlements and farms. However some of the woodland was low lying with a heavy cloying clay soil that they would have foreseen little advantage in clearing away. They would have left this for gathering wood. Later on this would have been managed which is where the coppicing would have come in. Priors Coppice has several giant coppice stools still remaining, some as large as 5 metres (16 feet) in diameter. These are believed to be several hundred years old.

As you may expect the flora and fauna of the coppice includes a vast range of specimens. The major trees are ash maple and ash wych-elm. Over 230 species of plants and ferns can be found here, with large colonies of wood anemone and purple orchid. Butterflies such as the orange tip and brimstone flit among the greenery while nuthatches, black caps and garden warblers swoop through the trees. Mammals are represented by all sizes from stoats to badgers.

50

From Priors Coppice the map tells me there is a bridleway. I have recollections of my previous struggle with this type of thoroughfare but am delighted to find that it is surfaced. The bridleway takes me downwards to the River Chater and provides wonderful views of the Chater valley. The surfaced bridleway continues up the other side of the valley and it very easy walking. My previous experiences with bridleways were being pushed to the back of my memory.

As the route started to take me over the hilltop and back down again the world underfoot suddenly changed. No sooner had I passed between a pair of stone gateposts than the curse of the bridleway struck again. The next downhill section was along a river of mud. Fortunately a wire fence provided me with some assistance to retain my balance as I squelched and slid my way to the end of the bridleway. A farm track appeared after about a quarter of a mile which made the next uphill stage to Belton-in-Rutland that much easier.

Belton-in Rutland and Allexton are virtually the same village, split by a short distance of road. The journey into Allexton crosses two lines. The visible line is formed by the A47 road slashing its way between the villages. The invisible line is the county boundary because it is time to say goodbye to the joys of Rutland to spend a short time in Leicestershire.

The Macmillan Way leads me over the gentle wolds of south east Leicestershire for the next three miles. I must give full marks for the way Leicester County Council have marked the footpaths. Large yellow posts act as a beacon for the stiles and gateways enabling the correct portals to be identified.

Hallaton

The village of Hallaton has a lovely village green which provides me with a pleasant location for a lunch break. The small green has two major features. The first is an unusual buttercross. It is constructed of local stone, conical in shape with a stone ball balancing on the point. I have not seen a market marker with such a shape before. I could not discover exactly when the buttercross was erected, but it is believed to date back to medieval times. The stone cross war memorial is a relatively more recent addition to the green. The whole green is set off with a backdrop of thatched stone cottages with bright flowers on their fronts. It is an ideal photo opportunity.

There is a well placed seat where I indulge in my lunch. Next to the seat is an information plaque telling me of the events that occur at Hallaton annually every Easter Monday

One of the great joys of visiting so many places in the countryside is that every now and again I come across some strange local customs. There is often a common thread to them in that at some point in the past the locals have overcome the treachery of their neighbours. This victorious achievement is celebrated annually with an unruly game which when all is said and done is usually just a good excuse for a bit of a bundle, followed by much drinking of alcoholic beverages. I was delighted to find that the "Hallaton Hare Pie Scramble and Bottle Kicking Festival" was no exception.

Local lore tells of two ladies of Hallaton who were attacked by a raging bull. Disaster was averted when a hare distracted the bull and the distraught ladies were able to escape to safety. The ladies were allegedly so grateful to God for sending the hare to save them that they donated a considerable sum of money to the church with the condition that on every Easter Monday the vicar served up a dish of Hare Pie to the villagers, along with a dozen loaves of bread and two barrels of beer. One cannot help but think that the poor hare came out of this rather badly.

There is an alternative version that the hare pie was originated as homage to the pagan god Oestre, but where is the fun in that one?

The bottle kicking goes back over 200 years. (Once again this is according to local custom). Whilst the good people of Hallaton were fighting over the portions of hare pie, their nasty neighbours from Medbourne sneaked into the village and stole away with the beer. The enraged Hallatonians put aside their squabbling over the food and co-operated to snatch the barrels back. The successful outcome was celebrated with much enthusiasm, and the game of bottle kicking was created to re-enact the triumphal battle.

The Easter Monday festival is held in two parts. First there is a procession from the Fox Inn, led by the Warrener with his hare-topped staff of office. He is escorted by his attendants who carry baskets of bread and also the traditional hare pie. The "bottles" are three wooden kegs decorated with ribbons, each barrel weighing 5kg. These kegs are carried by three men.

When the procession arrives at the church the pie is blessed, and it is then thrown to the crowd. The mad scramble to grab bits of pie begins! These days it is more symbolic than a genuine feast for the poor, and no doubt the local dogs among the crowd end up with all of the pieces of meat that find the ground.

The second part of the festival is the bottle kicking. The procession proceeds to Hare Pie Bank where the game is played. Each team will attempt to score goals by carrying a barrel across one of two streams that are a mile apart. The "bottles" are thrown into the air and it is game on! When each of the three bottles has crossed a stream the game is over. Apart from the manner in which a goal is scored there are no other rules except for a ban on gauging and the prohibition of weapons. Injuries are inevitable.

When the game has been completed it is a case of everybody back to the pub where the heroes of the day are celebrated in time honoured fashion.

Hallaton Treasure

Hallaton Treasure was discovered in 2000 after Ken Wallace and a team of enthusiasts first discovered some old pottery in surrounding fields. The area was examined by archaeology experts from Leicester University who uncovered over 5,000 gold and silver coins. A selection of the coins is exhibited in Market Harborough Museum.

Weston by Welland

By the time I cross the River Welland for the last time the river has considerably reduced in size from my first encounter with it out in the fenlands. Even with the swollen waters following the recent heavy rainfalls it is now a tiny waterway in comparison. This is not surprising considering that I have travelled over sixty miles since my first acquaintance with the river. I will now be leaving the River Welland behind. In fact it will be a considerable time before I encounter another of our major rivers although there are many small ones to be found in the Northamptonshire hills ahead.

Crossing the River Welland also takes me across the county border into Northamptonshire where I will be spending most of the next three and a half days.

Village Development

The small villages that I have passed through today and those that I will be passing through over the rest of my time in Northamptonshire all have a marked similarity. They are generally small, with a church and at least one "big house" of some description. This could range from a large stately home to a manor house. The villages are also primarily agricultural with only a few works units as additional sources of employment.

It is no surprise to learn that this similarity is mostly due to the way in which all of these places tended to develop over the centuries. Let me take this opportunity to outline the development of a typical village of this area. Remember that this is for the agricultural country area of Northamptonshire, Oxfordshire and Leicestershire. We will see later on that the Cotswolds developed in a very different manner being mostly influenced by the demand for wool and cloth.

Most of the Northamptonshire villages can trace their origins back to Saxon times. However, we have already seen that the Romans were prevalent in this region before then so it is very likely that when they departed the Saxons moved into some of their vacant farms. The early Saxon settlements were probably small clusters of farmsteads scattered across the countryside.

During the later Saxon years the people started to live in larger communities. There were probably three major factors that influenced this change. The first reason is that of security and defence. Our ancestors would have felt safer from marauding groups if they had strength in numbers. It was easier for outsiders to pillage and loot isolated dwellings.

The second reason is the introduction of Christianity. This is a difficult concept for us to understand today, but the church had a great influence on our forebears. Most people wanted to be near the church and so as the buildings were put up across the region the local people started to gravitate towards the church as the centre of their lives.

The final factor was the specialisation of labour and mutual dependency. As people learned that they gained overall by developing special skills and trading with each other instead of everyone trying to do everything themselves it made sense to group together to have access to those skills.

The arrival of William the Conqueror changed all that had gone before. William introduced the continental "feudal system" to England which was to be the way the country would be run until Henry VIII dissolved the monasteries in 1538.

A study of the feudal system would take a whole book in itself so I will keep to generalisations here. In its simplest form land was divided into three estates, nobility, clerical and vassal. The land was held by either the nobility or the clergy. They in turn leased it to the vassals, (often referred to as Lords of the Manor), who paid dues to them in the form of taxes, tithes and providing men at arms for the English armies. The vassals would employ the peasants (or serfs) to work for them.

As you can imagine, this resulted in the Lord of the Manor holding considerable power over the villagers. They were very much dependant on their Lords for employment because there was little other opportunity for work in the countryside. Freehold land was a great rarity.

This is how things were until the Dissolution of the Monasteries. The closures saw many of the estates of the great religious houses granted to the supporters of the King. Many country estates and manors were acquired shortly afterwards by the wealthier merchants, government officials and military generals.

Moving into the early 18th century life in most English villages followed a similar pattern. The Lord of the Manor was still in prime position, with the local vicar or rector often occupying the second-largest property for his vicarage. A whole raft of servants was required for the stately homes and the manor houses, particularly housekeepers, maids, laundry maids, cooks, grooms and stable hands. The Rector would usually have a minimum of housekeeper, cook and gardener while almost every farm would also have their own domestic servants. During the 18th and 19th centuries it would be common for 30% of the village to be employed in service.

During this period agriculture was still the major source of employment and more than half of the countryside population would have been employed in it.

While there are cases of some workers moving vast distances in general most people stayed where they were. Marriages tended to be localised, with the more adventurous seeking spouses from the surrounding villages. Village fairs and Feast Days were major social occasions and the young men and women would use these events to eye up the local talent.

Although life was hard for most people there does seem to have been more of a community spirit in the villages. It was expected for the Lord of the Manor and the Church to support the poor by offering employment and shelter.

The coming of the Industrial Revolution had a major effect on country life. Families deserted the countryside and flocked into the towns to take advantage of the opportunities of regular employment and higher wages in the factories. Another cause of people moving away from the countryside was the attraction to many people of a new life in the New World. We have already seen that the people of Boston, Lincolnshire emigrated to America in large numbers and this was repeated in many places across the country.

The trend of people, particularly the younger people, to leave their home villages continued into the mid-twentieth century when a remarkable reverse started to take place. People who had made some money in the towns started to move back into the countryside to escape from the busy towns. All of a sudden it became the "in thing" to move out of town into a quiet village.

From the villages being generally lower income they have become rather well-off again in many cases. Many of the residents of these villages I will be passing through over the next four days will be earning their money in places such as Leicester, Northampton, Kettering and Daventry. They will not be dependent on the inconsistencies of fortune from tending the crops as were their predecessors.

The wheel turns and we all move on.

BRAMPTON ASH TO MAIDWELL

Braybrooke

I am blessed with an easy start to the day with the benefit of a surfaced lane out of Brampton Ash followed by a good track through some woods. I am told that I may be fortunate enough to come across some grazing deer on this section, but despite keeping a good lookout I fail to come across any. It may well have been that my clumping feet through the otherwise quiet Northamptonshire countryside scattered any lurking deer well before I had the opportunity to set my eyes on them.

From Brampton Wood to Great Oxendon the Macmillan Way shares the right of way with the Jurassic Way. The latter is an 88 mile Northamptonshire County Path running between Stamford and Banbury following the line of the Jurassic limestone belt.

My path passes along the outside of Hermitage Wood, well known for its thick carpet of bluebells. With bluebells I am more fortunate. The deer may be able to run and hide from me but the bluebells are firmly fixed in the ground and cannot evade me. Indeed they present a wonderful display and the woodland to my right possesses a wash of blue under its leafy canopy.

The route twists a little in order to facilitate a reasonably safe place for walkers to cross the busy A6. With that task safely accomplished my next obstacle is the railway line. I am pleased to discover a convenient pass under the embankment. This is swiftly followed by a small bridge over the River Jordan. The song says that the River Jordan is muddy and wide, but this diminutive namesake is muddy and narrow. The rains have really coloured it up and the normal small stream resembles a thick brown soup forcing its way towards the River Welland.

There are some earth mounds to my right and these are all that remains today of the former Baybrooke Castle. In common with many other sites I have already encountered on this journey the name "castle" was used to describe a fortified manor house rather than a military stronghold. The original owners of this house were the Latimer family and there are records of the manor house and its fishponds being here in the 12th century. In 1304 Thomas de Latimer was granted a licence to fortify the house and he also took the opportunity to dig out a moat at the same time. Baybrooke was first recorded as a castle in 1361. The castle changed hands during the early part of the 15th century, but later fell into disrepair and the structure was demolished in 1633.

More fields follow and I work my way up to Waterloo Lodge where things could have gone better. There appeared to be a bit of a tangle with the way marking and at one point I ended up in a vegetable garden with no exit apart from the gate that I came in by. I checked the wooden gate and sure enough there was a way mark fixed to it. After wandering around for a few minutes I found a likely looking path and a quick check with the compass showed that it would go in approximately the right direction. Good; problem solved.

All seemed tickety-boo until I reached the old railway line which according to the guidebook I would be following for the rest of the day. When I say reached, I mean that the gravel track was only a few yards in front of me, but between me and the track was a muddy ditch, a spiky bramble hedge, a strip of saplings and an evil-looking barbed wire fence. I must have wandered somewhere to the side of the recognised path because I seemed to be more or less in the right place. Try as I could there was no way out of the field because of tight hedges and yet more barbed wire. It was a long way back to the farm so there was only one thing for it. I selected the least unattractive point and crawled my way through fence, ditch, brambles and thicket while dragging my rucksack behind me. After only a few scratches, hook-ups and muttered curses I scrambled out onto the disused railway line that provides the route for the Brampton Valley Way.

Brampton Valley Way

The Brampton Valley Way is described as a "linear nature reserve", which in easily translated terms means that an old derelict section of railway line has been cleared, given a bit of a poseur name and then opened to the public.

Brampton Valley Way provides a route between Little Cawden Crossing at Market Harborough and Broughton Crossing some 14 miles (22.5km) to the south in Northampton. It follows the old Market Harborough to Northampton railway line which was constructed to transport vast quantities of Northamptonshire ironstone from the quarries to the county town. The line was closed by the notorious Dr Beeching in the 1960's. Mind you, if Dr Beeching had not been such a butcher of the railways we would not have these wonderful walkways to enjoy today. Every cloud and all that.

Northamptonshire County Council received grant aid for the Brampton Valley way project from the Countryside Commission in 1987. The full track was opened in the spring of 1993.

I have to confess that I rather like walking along these old railway lines. They often offer either some splendid views from an embankment or a sheltered haven when enclosed by greenery on either side. On a more inclusive level they are also usually somewhere that both walkers and cyclists can share without getting too much into each other's way.

The Brampton Valley Way also offers another fairly unique experience and one which came as a total surprise. I know that preparation is everything, but when I am on these walks I like to take a lot of things as they come and do not spend too long analysing everything in advance. The rewards obtained from finding the unexpected for the first time usually outweigh any minor disadvantages. So when an initial reading of the guidebook said that there are tunnels on the route I admit that I did not take a lot of notice. I certainly did not think "I must take a torch". Mind you, if I had taken a torch I would have used it and missed out on a rather interesting experience.

The Great Oxendon Tunnel is 462 yards (422m) long and the entrance is just in front of me. It was designed and built by George Stephenson and opened in 1859. At the entrance I can see the small light of the tunnel exit in the far distance and hear the sound of water dripping from the roof into the puddles below. Everything else before me is black. After only a few steps into the blackness the light from the entrance behind me diminished rapidly and it became a case of moving steadily forwards towards the distant light. Only the sound of my footsteps told me what was underfoot, either the soft crunch of gravel or the splash of water. It was all rather spooky.

After a while my eyes became more accustomed to the dark and I could make out that some areas ahead of me were shiny black and other areas were matt black. I was soon able to determine that shiny black was puddle and matt black was tunnel. At a little over the halfway point a ventilation shaft in the roof aimed a pool of light onto the tunnel floor and enabled me to see some of the detail of the side walls. However, this was soon passed by and I continued my way steadily towards the growing archway of light ahead.

The last few dozen paces were into a continually brightening surround until I finally stepped out blinking into the bright sunshine. On reflection it was probably not that bright but it was still a very sharp contrast to the previous few minutes. The whole journey through the tunnel only took seven or eight minutes at the most but it was an interesting experience.

After the novel experiences of the tunnel the next three miles followed the old railway in an almost straight line with little variety in the flora inhabiting the borders. Young trees line both sides with the occasional gap allowing me a view across the adjacent fields. I reflect on the paradox of the tree-lined former railway track. When it was used for the purposes that it was designed for it is highly unlikely that trees would have been allowed to grow so close to the track and in many parts actually overhanging it. Sparks from the smokestack would have caused too many trackside fires. Therefore the track would have been open on either side. With no steam trains the trees could be permitted to grow again so giving us this lovely enclosed pathway to enjoy.

Approaching Kelmarsh the ground has been rising and soon in front of me there is another hill with a tunnel through it. I have arrived at the entrance to the slightly longer 530 yards Kelmarsh tunnel. Fortunately I am able to draw on my depths of experience of railway tunnel exploration and nonchalantly sashay my way into the darkness towards the beckoning arch of light in the distance.

Maidwell

I take my leave of the Brampton Valley Way shortly after the old Draughton Crossing. There is a sizeable car park here so anybody wishing to walk along the Brampton Valley Way starting from this point has simple access.

The Macmillan Way takes me uphill across two fields to the quiet stone village of Maidwell. After nearly eight miles of flat walking along the track the hill requires a little extra effort.

I emerge through a gate near to the church. The Church of Mary the Virgin has a squat, dumpy tower. The construction is mostly 13th and 14th century stonework. A little further along on the right there is a rather elegant 17th century stone gateway which was the former entrance to the gardens of Maidwell Hall.

Today the village of Maidwell has a population of around 330. There is evidence of people living here since the Bronze Age. Until the 7th century it was probable that this area was composed of a scattering of small farms dotted around the hillsides. After this time the people tended to move closer together to form a community. In later Saxon times there were two Manor Houses, on which the population were largely dependent. Gradually the two combined to form a single manor.

Another day's walking comes to an end. Today has been relatively quiet with most of the day spent on the former railway line that now carries the Brampton Valley Way. It is strange in a way. I am doing the walk to see the English countryside but the most powerful memories I will have of today is when I could see almost nothing apart from the speck of light at the end of the tunnel. Is there a subliminal message in there somewhere?

MAIDWELL TO FLORE

Maidwell to Creaton

This is the third day walking through Northamptonshire and it will be very much the same as the previous day. Northamptonshire is not one of the first counties that would be instantly recognised by many people as possessing a real "Olde England" landscape. I would bet that most people would straight away opt for Gloucestershire, Worcestershire or Wiltshire areas, but the merits of Northamptonshire far outweigh the common perception. There are some truly wonderful villages and because many of them are situated well off the beaten track they remain unspoiled by both modern development and the ravages inflicted by numerous visitors from the tourist industry. Today I will so closely approach Northampton that it hardly matters on the map, but on the ground it remains a world away from the hustle and bustle of the industrialised county town.

In the month of May the Northamptonshire agricultural countryside is almost entirely composed of four things, rapeseed, corn, cattle or sheep. The landscape is gently undulating, with nothing too high and nothing too steep. If you drop the occasional woodland and horse paddock into that scene it pretty much describes everything that lies between the many delightful stonework villages. If there was a "Goldilocks Zone" for countryside walking Northamptonshire would come as close as anywhere.

The first village that I encounter today is Cottesbrooke, which according to the last census has a population of 144. My brain immediately asks if this means that I can describe the local people as gross?

Cottesbrooke Hall was built in 1707 and is as near a perfect example of Queen Anne architecture as you could wish for. The front elevation of the house is almost perfectly symmetrical and is believed by many to have been the inspiration for Jane Austen's "Mansfield Park".

The next village that I pass through is Creaton which boasts an attractive village green and a much larger population of 486. After Creaton the Macmillan Way climbs steadily out of the valley and over the next ridge to join a country lane near to the hamlet of Teeton. My guidebook informs me that there is nothing to see at Teeton apart from a telephone box. I have seen one of these before so decided to give this (no doubt attractive) village a miss.

The Countryside Is Turning Yellow

William Blake wrote of "England's green and pleasant land". Well I have news for him. The land in this part of England is not green at this time of year. The land is bright yellow.

For the next few days the yellow peril will be a major feature of my daily life. May is the prime time for the rapeseed to be in its vivid flowering stage and everywhere I look swathes of fluorescent yellow fill the countryside.

This year presents more hassle than usual with traversing the fields of rapeseed. The weather has been so wet that many of the farmers have been unable to clear the footpaths through the fields, with the result that they have become overgrown with shoulder-high yellow rapeseed. Believe me this is a real struggle to push your way through. Each day my coat becomes covered in bright yellow flecks. Mark my words that a waterproof coat and over-trousers are absolutely essential in these conditions. Until you have pushed your way through a field of wet five-foot high rapeseed you will not know how soaked you can get!

The predominance of this crop is apparent wherever I look, but what are the reasons behind it being so plentiful? It is time to take a look at the world of rapeseed.

Brassica napus is the specific name for the rapeseed plant. It is a member of the mustard family. The common name of rapeseed is derived from the Latin *rapa* meaning turnip.

The commercial value is mainly in the vegetable oil obtained from the seed. Often the plant matter is ploughed back into the soil although it is edible. In some parts of the world it is eaten in a similar manner to spinach or kale.

Rapeseed oil is the third largest source of vegetable oil in the world, behind soya oil and palm oil. At one time the oil was only used as a lubricant due to high levels of glucosinolates and erucic acid which gave the oil a high acidity and a very bitter taste. These made the oil unsuitable even for animal feeds. Advances in plant breeding have led to varieties with most of the bitterness removed. One specific variety takes its name from the reduction of bitterness. It is known as Canola, which stands for CANadian Oil Low Acid.

The annual world production of rapeseed oil is in excess of 60 million tonnes, with the UK contributing over 2 million tonnes. The world's largest producers are China and Canada with 13 million tonnes and 11 million tonnes respectively.

The 1980's saw a massive increase in land being allocated for rapeseed. The principal reason was that the European Union offered huge subsidies for growing the crop.

One of the principle drivers across the world for rapeseed is its increasing use as a raw material for the production of "biodiesel". Over 65% of all rapeseed oil produced in Europe is currently processed into biodiesel.

If all this were not enough to encourage farmers to turn the countryside yellow the rapeseed oil is also alleged to have some health benefits over the use of other mineral oils. It only has 7% unsaturated fat compared to olive oil with 14%. Rapeseed also boasts a high vitamin E content, and as a further bonus it is also packed with those currently very trendy ingredients known as omega-3 and omega-6.

For a good harvest timing is absolutely critical. The pods have to be just right to give the maximum yield. Too early and the oil content is too low, but leave it too late and the fragile pods will have burst open scattering the seed before it can be collected by the farmer. Winter sown seed will usually be ready for harvesting in early August, while spring sown crops will be ready late August through to late September.

Oilseed rape appears to have established a very strong presence in the English countryside. The demand for more biodiesel is almost certain to increase the proportion of land put down to this crop. When it comes to springtime the future is yellow.

Holdenby

Holdenby is something a little different and the best way of describing it is to call it an "Estate Village". The well-kept houses all have immaculately maintained lawns and gardens. There is an overwhelmingly peaceful atmosphere with only the purring of a lone lawn-mower breaking the background of birdsong.

Holdenby is named after Richard Holdenby who was the Lord of the manor during the early 14th century. At that time Holdenby was a typically quiet manorial village.

The big change came during 1583 when Sir Christopher Hatton, the Chancellor to Elizabeth I, built a grand house on the estate. Sir Christopher was one of Elizabeth's favourite courtiers. His popularity combined with skilful political manoeuvring enabled him to rise through the government offices and accrue great wealth.

Hatton was a major investor in the activities of Francis Drake, and as a consequence became a major beneficiary of Drake's pirate activities in Spanish America. So grateful was Drake for Hatton's investment that he changed the name of his ship to "Golden Hind" in recognition of the gold deer displayed on the Hatton coat of arms.

Armed with his considerable financial reserves Hatton set his ambition towards building the grandest individual house in England. In an era where glass was very expensive Sir Christopher deliberately built a mansion with 123 windows so that it displayed a testimony to his great wealth. So determined was Hatton to have the perfect house that he even moved every cottage in the village to a new location so that it did not spoil the view from the house.

Sir Christopher Hatton was so devoted to the service of his Queen that he refused to live in the house until Elizabeth herself had visited the stately edifice. The more cynical among us could say that this was crawling to the ultimate degree.

Hubris was to be his downfall. Hatton may have built the most marvellous house in England but, like so many like him before and since, the sheer cost of the building combined with the upkeep eventually bankrupted him. In the end he did not have long to enjoy his status symbol as he died soon afterwards in 1591. The Holdenby estate was eventually purchased by the crown in 1607 during the reign of King James I.

Earlier on my journey I discovered that King Charles I had been betrayed and captured during his stay at Stamford. Holdenby House is where the Roundheads brought him after he was taken prisoner. It was here that the King was first imprisoned, spending five months at Holdenby between February and June 1647. At the end of this period Charles I was taken from Holdenby to Newmarket by George Joyce and handed over to Cromwell's New Model Army. Charles was later moved around several other houses before his trial and execution at Whitehall on January 30th 1649.

Holdenby House eventually passed into the hands of Captain Adam Baynes who demolished most of the original building, leaving only a small domestic wing standing.

In 1709 the house and estate were purchased by the Marlborough family, who in turn sold it on to the Clifdens, from where it descended through the distaff line to the Lowther family who are still the incumbent owners. It was the Clifden family who were responsible for rebuilding the house in 1873. They added further extentions to the structure in 1878. As large as it is today it is incredible to visualise that the current house is only about one eighth of the size of Hatton's palatial symbol of wealth. Two arches and a kitchen area are all that remains of the original structure of Holdenby House.

A short diversion along the road is required for me to view Holdenby House. On setting eyes on it I realise that I have seen this house before, but it was not in this well maintained state. The last time I saw this building was on the 2011 BBC film of "Great Expectations". In order to obtain the desired effect the set designers had spent four days and utilised 80 tonnes of mud, weed and creepers to transform this building into the decrepit "Satis House", the home of the reclusive Miss Haversham.

Holdenby Church

A further short diversion is required to pay a visit to Holdenby Church. This building is all that remains of the site of the original village from Richard Holdenby's time. Even Sir Christopher Hatton did not dare to risk offending the higher powers by moving the church.

All Saints Church is a grade II listed building first commissioned by Richard Holdenby in 1330. The chancel was rebuilt by Sir Henry Drysden in 1843 and the whole church was extensively restored under the direction of Sir George Gilbert Scott between 1867 and 1868.

On the walls of the nave are seven painted panels. The panels contain texts from the Bishops Bible of 1568 and are thought to date from the Elizabethan era. The church also contains an alabaster floor memorial dedicated to William Holdenby who died in 1490. Another interesting feature is the choir stalls. These were originally used in Lincoln Cathedral and were made during the 15th century.

In 1972 the parish of Holdenby was united with the neighbouring parish of East Haddon and All Saints Church was declared redundant. Holdenby Church is now administered by the Churches Conservation Trust.

Althorp

The Macmillan Way takes the route along a country lane for the next three miles. On the left hand side of the lane is the northwest boundary wall of the Althorp Estate. It is a shame that a route cannot be found that takes in the estate because the grounds are quite striking.

Althorp covers approximately 14,000 acres (60 km^2). The estate is owned by Earl Charles Spencer, who is the nineteenth successive generation of his family to own the estate. The estate is however probably better known as being the ancestral home of Lady Diana Spencer, Princess of Wales. (1961-1997).

The Spencer family acquired the Althorp estate from the Catesby family in 1508. Sir John Spencer had amassed a huge wealth from sheep rearing in Warwickshire and used the fortune to establish the estate at Althorp.

The estate stands on a terrain of gently rolling hills with more than 1,000 acres of deciduous tree plantations. Over 500 acres of the estate are set out as parkland. The oldest tree in the park is a 72 feet high oak known as the Crimea Oak, planted by Sir John Spencer in 1589. It was part of a project by John Spencer to grow sufficient oak trees to replace the timber ships lost to the ravages of the Spanish Armada during the previous year. There is also a much newer avenue of thirty six oak trees planted by the current Earl Spencer in 1999. This avenue was planted as a memorial to Lady Diana. The thirty six trees are to commemorate the thirty six years of her life.

More than 3,000 acres are devoted to farmland. These working lands are managed in order to maintain a pleasant balance between commerce and conservation. There is a mixture of animal and arable and an active hedgerow management policy to enable wildlife to thrive.

There is a small lake known rather paradoxically as "The Round Oval". Situated in the centre of the lake is a small island which is the resting place of the late Princess of Wales. The spot is marked by a tasteful memorial stone designed by Edward Bulmer. The memorial was carved by Dick Reid.

The house was commissioned by Robert Spencer, 2nd Earl of Sunderland, in 1688. The Spencer's were previously at Wormleighton, Warwickshire until their 16th century manor house was burned down by the Royalists during the Civil War. The family then moved to their other estate at Althorp. Wormleighton Manor is still owned by the Spencer family.

Althorp House is not visible from this road. It is open for visitors from July 1st to 30th August every year. The original house was constructed in red-brick Tudor style. The architect Henry Holland made alterations to this from 1788.

The interior of the house boasts many fine rooms. Centrepiece is a wide wooden staircase dating back to 1666. With the same family living in the house for some 500 years a great collection of portraits and artifacts has been accumulated over the centuries and there are many fine original works to be seen on display.

It may seem rather odd, but the stable block is a more attractive building than the house itself. Both are Grade I listed buildings but the stables definitely have the edge. The stables have a Palladian style appearance. The building was constructed in the 1730's from the local honey coloured ironstone. The stable block is deemed to display the best architecture of the whole estate. This elegant structure is now the home of an exhibition dedicated to the life of Lady Diana Spencer.

The Domesday Book records the village of Althorp, but there is no settlement on the estate today. In fact there has not been a village is one of those mysterious "lost villages". At one point they are thriving, and in the next report there is nobody living there. The likelihood is that it was Catesby who, for whatever reason he had, cleared the village of its inhabitants. Records dating from 1505 state that there were no residents at that time.

The Bringtons

The next three miles of The Macmillan Way follow the road through the villages of Great Brington and Little Brington. Great Brington is a pleasant mixture of stone, brick and thatch. The church and adjoining rectory provide a welcoming entrance to the village from my direction of approach. Opposite to the church is a small raised village green with a giant horse chestnut tree in the centre. There is also a welcoming wooden bench which provides me with a short rest.

The spire of Little Brington church is visible from quite some way away but when I reach the building I have something of a surprise. There in front of me is the spire, but something is definitely missing. It's the church!

All that remains today of Little Brington church is the spire. The church of St John was built here in the mid-19th century as a chapel of ease for the villagers of Little Brington and Nobottle to save them from travelling to Great Brington.

By 1940 the church had seen better days and was steadily falling into decay. Finally in 1947 the church was closed and doomed to demolition. The reason that the spire is still here today comes from an unlikely source. The Air Ministry declared that the distinctive octagonal spire was extremely useful as a navigation aid because it was clearly distinguishable from long distances. This insistence from the Air Ministry led to the result that the rest of the church was demolished leaving the spire untouched. It was then able to devote all of its energies into fulfilling its new purpose in directing lost airmen back to base.

Navigation aids have come a long way since then and I doubt whether any stray descendant of Biggles has had cause to thank the Ministry for retaining the spire in recent years. For my part it tells me that I am exactly 96 miles along the Macmillan Way and there are 3 miles left to cover today.

M1 Motorway

Leaving the solitary spire behind I enter another series of the all pervasive fields of yellow rapeseed. The Macmillan Way takes me on a tour round the edges of several of these fields and all I can see to either side is a sea of yellow.

The path dips down and passes some fishing pools before rising a little towards the next summit, where I come across a totally different beast altogether. The familiar drone becomes louder and louder until it has turned into a deep roar and I am standing on a bridge looking down on the M1.

Motorways are an essential bane of our lives. They are noisy, dusty, and full of choking diesel fumes. Not to mention being the source of endless frustrations with their all-too-frequent traffic jams. All that said they still provide the most convenient way of travelling between two places that we have so far devised.

Who was responsible for the motorway as we know it? Most people would instinctively accuse the Americans while others would go for the Germans with their Autobahns. It came as a surprise to me that the answer is that the first Motorways were built by the Italians under the instructions of Mussolini in 1924. They were followed by the autobahns of Adolf Hitler in the 1930's.

Britain was not as far behind with this development as you may first think. As we often find when we look at these things closely somebody had the idea but government procrastination and red-tape hindered progress. Things were just as bad then as they are now. Lord Montague founded a company in 1923 to build a motorway from London to Birmingham but he could not penetrate through all the bureaucracy. It was not until the passing of the Special Roads Act in 1949 that motorways restricted to certain classes of vehicles were able to obtain government approval.

The M1 was the first motorway to be completed in Britain. It was opened by Transport Minister Ernest Marples on November 2nd 1959. Quiz buffs will point out that the M1 was not the first motorway section to be used, because that honour goes to the Preston By Pass (now part of the M6) which was opened by Harold MacMillan in 1958.

The initial M1 was a 62 mile stretch from Berrygrove, Watford (now Junction 5) to Crick (now Junction 18). The route followed the approximate line of the A5 and was constructed by two companies, Tarmac Construction (Junctions 5 to 10) and John Laing (Junctions 10 to 18). The initial cost of the motorway was £26 million, which would equate to £400 million at today's (2012) prices.

In the early days there were no speed limits on the motorway, with the 70 mph limit not being introduced until 1967. The cars driven by many people in those times simply could not cope with the demands made upon them by their drivers. The vast majority of the early breakdowns on the M1 were due to the engines overheating. It was a common sight to see vehicles on the hard shoulder with their bonnets raised and steam gushing from the engine compartment. Advances in engine technology have resulted in this problem being almost eliminated. Reports from the AA now are that 26% of all motorway breakdowns are due to tyre failure. With the cost of towing a breakdown off the motorway that is a very good reason to check tyre wear and pressures before making long motorway journeys.

The M1 today is more than three times longer than the original motorway, stretching 193.6 miles (311km) from London to the A1(M) at Aberford, just north of Leeds.

The section that I am crossing now has an average daily flow of approximately 100,000 vehicles per day. It is amazing that this figure is reached at all because the engineers who designed the original motorway calculated that it could cope with 20,000 vehicles per day. The whole M1 has a total usage of over 140,000 vehicles per day. It is horrifying to be told that without modifications to the motorway the anticipated increase in traffic will see most sections reduced to stop-start flows by 2025. (AA estimation).

Flore

Flore is situated only just off the M1 but is a remarkably quiet village. This is probably due to the motorway being in a cutting which keeps the traffic noise contained.

Flore is the largest place that I have encountered since leaving Oakham. The current population is around 1200 in number.

I make my way through the village streets to All Saints Church which marks my end point for today. The church stands in a very traditional churchyard with yew trees providing both an attractive screen for the church but also a shady canopy for the graveyard. From the churchyard gate I can see across the Nene Valley to the hills of South Northamptonshire beyond. The landscape before me is my destination for tomorrow. I hear that Mother Nature spreads her cloak on the countryside. From what I can see lays ahead of me she has covered South Northamptonshire in a hi-viz jacket!

FLORE TO CHIPPING WARDEN

DAY 7

16 MILES

River Nene

Coming out of Flore the Macmillan Way descends slightly to cross the early reaches of the River Nene. This part of the path is shared with the Nene Way, which runs from the source at Badby to Wansford, Cambridgeshire.

The Nene is probably one of this country's lesser known rivers, but in fact it is the tenth longest river in the United Kingdom. It is almost exactly 100 miles (161km) long from its source at Arbury Hill near Badby, Daventry to entering the sea at The Wash. On its journey to the sea the River Nene passes through Northampton, Wellingborough, Irthlingborough, Thrapston, Oundle and Peterborough. The last 88 miles of the river from Northampton to the sea are navigable.

The pronunciation of the name of the river is subject to local variation. The upper river is generally pronounced "Nenn" (to rhyme with pen), while the lower reaches around Peterborough are usually referred to as "Neen" (as in queen) by the locals there. If we take this division literally then somewhere around the Thrapston area there will be two next-door neighbours who spend all of their time arguing about which is the correct pronunciation to use.

Soon after crossing the Nene I also pass over the Grand Union Canal and the main Euston to Birmingham railway line. Almost immediately afterwards there is a significant milestone on my expedition but there is nothing that visibly marks the point. I have now completed 100 miles of the Macmillan Way.

Birth of Radar

The climb up to the pretty village of Church Stowe is probably the steepest incline since I tackled the slippery gradient up to Easton on the Hill on day three. Effort reaps its own rewards and looking back across the valley I can see a beautiful English countryside scene with extensive views across the fledgling Nene valley.

A little way over on Borough Hill I can see a communication mast. It is the proximity of this mast combined with the suitability of Church Stowe as an observation point that made this particular location the place where great advances were made in the science of navigation.

During the early 1930's the boffins at the National Physical Laboratory were fairly sure from their researches that the phenomenon we know today as radar (RAdio Detection And Ranging) was theoretically possible. They had just not yet been able to prove that it was achievable in practice. On the morning of February 26th 1935 all that was to change.

Arnold Frederick Wilkins and Robert Watson Watt had set up their monitoring oscilloscope in a field just outside Church Stowe. The experiment that they would conduct would be to monitor the 49 metre wavelength signal from the Marconi/BBC mast at Borough Hill. At a pre-arranged time an aeroplane would fly overhead. Their theory was that the passing of the aircraft would cause interference to the electromagnetic energy fields broadcast from the mast and that they could use this distortion of the energy wave to track the position of the aircraft.

The aeroplane was a Handley Page Heyford biplane number K6902. It was piloted by Flt.Lt.Robert Blake (1897–1988). Blake was later to rise during the war through the senior levels of the RAF to gain the rank of Air Vice-Marshall.

To the great delight of Wilkins and Watt there was not only interference of the electromagnetic field, but they were also able to track the position of the biplane for a further distance of eight miles. This was far more than they had dared to hope for with this first attempt. Radar detection was practically proven and would be rapidly developed to become an important mechanism for the future defence of the nation from air attack.

In September 2001 a memorial stone dedicated to this event was unveiled. It is situated on the side of the A5 just to the south of the nearby village of Weedon.

Farthingstone

It does not appear evident to me now, but the approach to Farthingstone passes by the site of a former hill fort known as Castle Dykes. From the Macmillan Way it does not look clear that the fort was ever there, certainly nowhere near the definition of the hill forts that I will encounter later when I reach the Cotswolds. The area to the northeast of Farthingstone has also produced evidence of an ancient longbarrow.

Today, however, there is clear evidence that quite a few people genuinely believe that something used to be here, and that there are undiscovered delights still buried in the fields. There are people swarming all over the fields and at first glance I could be forgiven for thinking that they are hoovering the fields whilst listening to their favourite rock band on a set of headphones. Closer inspection reveals that they are all wielding metal detection kits and are diligently searching for ancient artefacts. I have stumbled upon an organised treasure hunt and it does seem to be very popular. Good luck to them all.

The village of Farthingstone has a population of 179 according to the 2001 census. In the Domesday Book the settlement is given the title of Fordinstone. The village was given to the Earl of Moreton by his half-brother, William the Conqueror. Who said that connections don't help?

Walking along Main Street towards the church there is a wrought iron gate set into a stone archway to my left. Hidden behind this gate is Farthingstone's secret place; the Joy Mead Gardens.

Immediately through the gate there is a large lawn. To the left of the greensward there is a small stone temple and to the right there is a cloistered area. Further down the side of the lawn a children's' play area can be seen.

The Joy Mead Gardens were bequeathed to the village of Farthingstone in 1922 by the Agnew family who lived at Littlecourt in the village.

Philip Agnew was born in 1864 and was educated at Rugby School and New College Oxford. After graduating in Classics and Modern History he was called to the Bar in Lincolns Inn. Instead of following a career in the law Philip decided instead to join the family business of Bradbury Agnew and Company who were printers and publishers. The company printed and published a wide range of books and periodicals. During their expansion Bradbury Agnew acquired the popular humorous magazine "Punch". Philip Agnew became Managing Director of the celebrated publication.

Agnew was also an excellent pianist and developed close connections with the Royal College of Music. He became Chairman of the Governing Body, a position he served with distinction for sixteen years. Philip was also a local Magistrate and was appointed as High Sherriff of Northamptonshire in 1924-5.

While his business and public life were highly successful Philip Agnew's private life was rather sad. He married his wife, Alexandra (but known to everyone as Georgette) Christian in 1899. Initially they set up home in London, but in 1910 moved to Littlecourt in Farthingstone.

Their first daughter, Christine, died during childhood in 1896. The second child, Enid Jocelyn (known as Joy) married Roger Evans and bore a child, Michael, in 1920. Unfortunately Joy contracted TB shortly after the birth and died within a year. Michael himself sadly died on active service in the Middle East during 1942.

Philip and Georgette's son, Ewan, also died at a young age. He contracted an illness during the Great War and lived in poor health until his eventual passing in 1930.

Work started on the Joy Mead Gardens early in 1922. They were opened on August 3rd of that year and formally dedicated to the memory of Joy. It was the expressed wish of the Agnew family that the gardens should be used by the people of the village for recreation and as a safe playground for local children. It was also their wish that the uses should include concerts, dramas, dances and other social functions.

The cloistered area was built following the death of Ewan Agnew. There is a stone tablet in the cloister area dedicated to Ewan and all others who died either directly or indirectly as a result of the Great War.

Philip Agnew died in March 1938 following a prolonged period of illness. Georgette continued to live in the family home at Littlecourt until she passed away in 1958. The Agnews considered that Littlecourt was ill-fated to be a house of sadness and did not want that sorrow to be passed on to any future tenants. To ensure an end to any such unwanted legacies the house was demolished in 1960.

It is a dull day today and only one other person has come to sit in the garden while I have been here. I can imagine that on a warm summer evening things are very different with young children burning off their surplus energy within these delightful enclosed gardens.

Canons Ashby

Augustinian Monks wore distinctive black habits and acquired the sobriquet of "Black Canons". Ashby means "farmstead" so Canons Ashby translates simply as the farmstead of the Augustinian Monks.

The Augustinians first moved here to start building their Priory during the 12th century. Although they were relatively small in numbers they made up for this with their great dedication and over the following years constructed a sizeable priory and church. As was common in those days a small village soon developed around the priory to service the requirements of the monastery and its farmland. The priory also became a popular stopping off point for pilgrims on their travels, and was particularly popular with students from Oxford University. The future looked assured for Canons Ashby.

Then, during the 14th century, came the arrival of the Black Death. The deadly plague swept across Europe leaving devastation and abandoned villages in its wake. Canons Ashby was badly affected by the fatal disease and the priory crashed into rapid decline. At its lowest point there were only thirteen monks in a fit state to cover all of the essential tasks of the monastery.

Somehow the priory managed to limp along and survive. That is until the "Dissolution of the Monasteries" by Henry VIII in 1536. Canons Ashby was one of the first monasteries to be evacuated and the Black Canons were forced to leave. The Priory and its surrounding lands were given to Sir Francis Bryson by Henry VIII.

The construction of the present manor house began around 1550 and was commissioned by John Dryden. Dryden had inherited (through marriage) a farmhouse which he gradually developed into a fine manor house. The materials for the house were obtained from ransacking the nearby Priory. The house and interior design remain virtually unchanged since 1710 although there has been much restoration work required over the years in order to maintain the appearance.

Canons Ashby has been under the management of the National Trust since 1981. There is still remedial work being carried out here to bring the restoration work up to date. At the time of my visit an update of the gardens had only recently been completed, copying drawings made during the early 18th century.

Much of the restoration work has only been possible due to the incredible records kept by Sir Henry Dryden. He was known as "The Antiquary" and was totally besotted with recording the intricate details of architecture and design. Sir Henry inherited Canons Ashby in 1837 and was the custodian through most of the Victorian era. He kept the most immaculate records of everything connected with the house and gardens. These studies have helped the National Trust immensely with the restoration work. The inside of the house boasts fine plasterwork and decorative Jacobean paintings and tapestries. It is well worth a visit.

The church is also worth calling into. It is set a couple of hundred yards away from the house and is all that is left standing of the former priory. Inside the church there are memorials to the Dryden family and also there are information panels detailing the history of the church and priory.

The National Trust kindly allows Macmillan Way walkers to use the gravel path through the grounds of the house without paying the entrance fee. Not only does this provide me with superb views of the rear of the house and the gardens, coupled with an excellent view of the church with its tower through the parkland trees, but it also passes the tea-room with its welcoming display of cakes. It would be criminal not to stop.

Moreton Pinkney

Now there's a funny name for a village.

Mor meaning farmland and ton meaning enclosure or homestead is derived straight from the Anglo Saxon. So what about Pinkney?

In common with most places in England following the Battle of Hasting the lands were taken by William the Conqueror and redistributed to his friends and supporters. One such fortunate recipient was Gilo de Pinchegni, formerly a resident of Picardy. After the Norman invasion Gilo de Pinchegni was installed as Lord of the Manor of Moreton. It must have been so much easier for the rulers to gain loyal support in those days. "Help me and I will make you Lord of the Manor" seems so much more persuasive than "Vote for me and I might consider knocking 1p off income tax". It may also have helped that William obviously kept his promises to his followers.

The manor stayed in the hands of the de Pinchegni family for 260 years, from 1086 until 1346, when the estate was sold.

It is the sixth generation descendant of Gilo who made the most significant contribution to English history. Robert de Pinkney (see how the name had altered over the years) was one of the original signatories to Magna Carta at Runnymede in 1215.

Eydon

Eydon. What does the name bring to mind? Garden of Eden? Former Prime Minister Anthony Eden? Ginormous greenhouses in rural Cornwall? Whatever thoughts have raced through your mind I will bet that they are still a long way away from kettles!

Eydon is the home of the Eydon Storm Kettle Company. This kettle is an ingenious little device that allows the intrepid explorer to boil water wherever he (or she) may be.

The kettle was originally developed on the west coast of Ireland where they used specially adapted copper vessels. The design has been improved by Eydon resident John Grindlay, who runs the company from his home in the village.

Let me describe the Eydon kettle. Imagine a metal can 12 inches (30cm) high and 6 inches (16cm) diameter similar in appearance to a miniature milk churn. Then add a pouring spout towards the top. The centre is a hollow conical tube, wide at the bottom and narrower at the top. This forms an outer boiling chamber and the water is poured into this outside chamber of the can. The can is then placed on a vented metal dish, with the tube forming a chimney.

The fuel can be anything that will burn. Paper is required to get a fire started, but then the fuel can be anything combustible. I played with "google" and discovered some instructions on the web site that suggested using twigs, cones, grass and even camel dung! Additional fuel can be dropped into the top of the cone as required. The heat from the miniature bonfire rapidly warms the water from the inside of the boiler and before you know it you can have up to 1.5 litres of boiling water for a cup of tea, even in the most inhospitable weather conditions.

The kettles are available at the time of writing (2012) at £49.95 each. Further details including a cut-away drawing showing how it all works is available online at www.eydonkettle.com

There are a full range of accessories that can be purchased online, but you will need to find your own camel.

Chipping Warden

My house is just a little to the east of Banbury. The village of Chipping Warden is only a ten minutes drive from where I live. This is the closest that the Macmillan Way comes to my home.

There is an excellent pub in Chipping Warden called "The Griffin" so guess where I have planned to end my route today? As I approach the outskirts of the village I pull my mobile out of my pocket and contemplate my options.

I have a problem. I could phone now and "Dearly Beloved" would almost certainly be waiting for me by the time I approached the village green. If I phoned when I actually arrived at "The Griffin" I would have about ten minutes to wait, during which time I could occupy myself with a beer to while away the time. Life is full of decisions. By the time I had reached the threshold of the welcoming door of the hostelry I had decided that a really unscrupulous person would phone to say that he had only just got there after he had ordered his second (or even third) pint. Problem solved.

CHIPPING WARDEN TO EPWELL

DAY 9

14 MILES

Oxford Canal

Just before reaching the village of Claydon the Macmillan Way crosses over the Oxford Canal. In my personal view the Oxford Canal is one of England's most attractive inland waterways.

The canal covers 78 miles (126km) from the River Thames in Central Oxford to the Coventry Canal at Hawkesbury Junction, Bedworth. A few miles to the north of where I am now, between Broughton and Napton Junction, the Oxford Canal shares its waters with the Grand Union Canal that links London and Birmingham.

The construction of the Oxford Canal was championed by Sir Roger Newdigate (1719-1806) who was the Member of Parliament for Oxford University. Permission to start the work was granted by a 1769 Act of Parliament. The chief designer and engineer was the noted canal constructor James Brindley. Following Brindley's death in 1772 the project was completed by his brother-in-law Samuel Simcock.

Things were essentially no different in those days for major construction projects than they are today. The work started at the Coventry end and by 1774 had only reached Napton before – you have guessed it - the project ran out of money. It required a second Act of Parliament to be passed in 1775 in order to generate more funds before work was able to continue. The canal was then extended to Banbury which it reached in 1778. At this point it was quickly realised that the only way that the canal would ever be completed to link with the River Thames was to construct the remaining 30 miles to Oxford "on the cheap". Even with all of the "cutting of the corners" and generally muddling through it was not until 1786 that the Oxford Canal was finally connected to the River Thames at Oxford.

The Oxford Canal was fairly unique among inland waterways in that it twisted and turned between the hills. At times it almost seems to come back on itself in great loops. There are some stretches where contouring around the hills added many extra miles to the journey. This led to several later projects that attempted to straighten out some of these sections. Fortunately for us much of the canal remains true to its original layout which adds tremendously to the beauty of the waterway.

Traffic on the canal consisted mostly of coal mined from the Warwickshire coalfields travelling south, with stone and agricultural products moving northwards. The opening of the Grand Union Canal in 1805 caused some reduction in usage because it enabled faster transport to London. It also enabled bargees to avoid using the River Thames where the hazardous "flash locks" were still in widespread use.

The Oxford Canal remained profitable right up to the nationalisation of the waterways in 1948 and well into the 1950's after that. Even so decline was to set in as it did with the rest of the canal transport system. By the time the early 1960's were with us commercial traffic had become almost non-existent on the southern part of the canal between Banbury and Oxford.

The Oxford Canal can boast that it had the last commercial working horse-drawn barge on the English canal system. The barge "Friendship" was pulled by a mule until 1959. "Friendship" can now be seen on public display at the National Waterway Museum in Ellesmere Port.

The Oxford Canal may have declined for the transportation of goods, but after surviving an attempt to close it during the latter 1960's the waterway has thrived with the boom in leisure activity. The narrow twisting waterway with its open views across the Oxfordshire and Warwickshire countryside, interspersed with short tree-lined sections and passing through attractive stone villages has become one of the most popular locations for waterborne holidays in the country. Simply crossing the bridge at Claydon gives a good impression of the beauty of the waterway and increases the desire to explore more of it.

Farnborough Hall

Crossing the Oxford Canal represents another change in the nature of the walk. The terrain is about to become much more hilly.

To the north of Banbury there is an undulating area known as the Burton Dassett Hills, taking the name from the small village of Burton Dassett.

The Burton Dassett Hills are a series of rugged hilltops that due to their isolated location afford spectacular views in every direction of the compass. The highest point is Magpie Hill which stands at 666feet (203metres) above sea level. The hills are formed from ironstone and are still quarried for the local stone.

The stone village of Farnborough sits on the southern edge of the Burton Dassett Hills and to reach this settlement requires a short climb. This sharp incline is the first in a series of many that I am going to encounter over the next few days.

The honey-coloured local stone bestows Farnborough Hall with a warm and welcoming glow from. It is built in the Palladian style with sash windows and a balustrade roof.

The estate was purchased by the Holbech family in 1684, with the house being constructed between 1745 and 1750. Although the Holbech family still reside at the Hall, ownership was passed to the National Trust in 1960.

Farnborough Hall boasts some superb examples of 18th century Rococo plasterwork including a very ornate domed ceiling. These fine works are by William Perritt and depict natural beauty and wildlife.

The Italianate hallway is an interesting feature of this house. There are oval niches on the walls displaying busts of Roman Emperors. The drawing room contains fine stucco work with scrolls, shells, fruit and flowers making up an impressive display. Copies of the paintings of Canaletto and Panini are exhibited in the dining room. The originals have long been sold, but the copies lose none of the grandeur of the room, even if the fiscal value is somewhat lowered.

The gardens were designed and landscaped by Sanderson Miller. There is a lake, terraced walk and several other pathways through the grounds. An Ionic Temple and an obelisk add to the attraction.

Warmington

Warmington is the first village that I come to that is classified as being within the "Cotswolds Area of Outstanding Natural Beauty".

The parish church has an unusual name being dedicated to "St. Peter ad Vincula". The Latin translates as "St. Peter in chains". I had not heard of this particular title before so was not too surprised to discover that there are only 15 churches in the whole of the UK with this dedication. The most celebrated of them is the Chapel Royal of St Peter ad Vincula, which is probably better known as the Chapel of the Tower of London.

The biblical significance can be found in Acts of the Apostles, Chapter 12 Verses 3 to 19. The story begins with Peter being arrested, chained and imprisoned by King Herod. On the night before his trial Peter was visited in his cell by an angel who instructed him to leave. At this point the restraining chains fell away and the cell door swung open. The angel guided Peter out of the prison and into the city before suddenly disappearing from view. Peter found his way to the house of Mary, the mother of John Mark where he was let into the residence by the servant girl Rhoda. The story ends with verse 19 where we are told that when Herod learned of the escape he ordered the prison guards to be put to death in punishment for their laxity.

My own exit from Warmington was not easy either. The stepped path beside the church rises very steeply up the hillside and seems to just keep on rising forever. There is a thoughtfully placed wooden bench at the top onto which I gratefully slump my puffing frame and reach into my rucksack for my water bottle.

Ratley and Edgehill

I am on an elevated position at the northern tip of the Cotswold Hills and the next four miles will provide me with elevated views right across the Avon Valley. To the northwest are the Burton Dassett Hills.

The Macmillan Way crosses several fields before arriving in the small sheltered village of Ratley. The fields give me another opportunity to do battle with wet rapeseed.

Just around the corner from the church there is a flight of steps with a cast iron handrail descending to my left. I drop down the steps to come to the Gogg's Spring, a natural spring that trickles into a brick surround. This spring is part of the Ratley Millennium Elements Trail.

To celebrate the Millennium the parishioners set up a small trail covering the ancient elements of earth, air, fire and water. The Gogg's Spring represents water. Air is represented twice, firstly by a weathervane on the gable of the village hall. The vane depicts a foot soldier carrying a spear and shield. The spear points out the direction of the wind. The second representation is the "airy seat of Ratley Castle". This mound is all that remains of an old "motte and bailey" castle built to protect the de Arden family during the turbulent reign of King Stephen. The castle building was later to be demolished by King Henry II in 1154.

The tribute to fire can to be found in the lower part of the recreation ground. The location is that of the village bonfire for the annual Guy Fawkes Night celebration. Near to the bonfire are stones marking the site of a time capsule intended to provide a future generation with "a unique account of the life and history of Ratley at the dawn of the third millennium". The capsule was buried on Midsummer Day, June 21st 2001.

Earth is represented by a stone obelisk that I discover as I leave the village. It is situated at the junction of the lane leading to Edgehill. The obelisk is inscribed at the top with "MM", the Roman numeral for 2000, plus the names of the three villages that make up the Parish, Ratley, Edgehill and Upton. The obelisk was allegedly constructed by the first female apprentice stonemason at the nearby Horton Quarry.

I will be turning to the southwest to follow the scarp slope for the next three miles. Most of this slope is heavily wooded so the views across the Avon Valley towards Stratford upon Avon will become intermittent through gaps in the trees. I had expected this path to be another muddy slog but it is in surprisingly good condition.

After about a mile the path takes me uphill and emerges at the Castle Inn at Edgehill. This unusual inn was originally built as a folly in 1742 by Stamford Miller, an 18th century gentleman architect who lived at the nearby Radley Grange. It is constructed from the local Horton stone. The distinguishing feature is a castellated tower rising above the rooftop giving it the outward appearance of a castle. The inn allegedly marks the spot where King Charles I raised the Royal Standard before the Battle of Edgehill in 1642. The folly has been in service as an inn since 1822.

This part of the escarpment is at a height of 700 feet (215 metres) and the terrace of the Castle Inn provides an excellent view over the area where the Civil war battle took place. The Castle Inn provides an excellent menu and also provides accommodation. Two of the bedrooms are in the tower, and are furnished with four-poster beds.

There are also many tales of ghostly apparitions in this area. The restless spirits of the Royalists and Parliamentarians are alleged to fight their battles over and over again while the rest of us sleep in our beds. During my researches I discovered a reference to the Edgehill ghosts as being one of the very few supernatural occurrences that are recorded at the Public Records Office. I think I will leave it there and continue on my travels before any see-through pikemen appear!

Battle of Edgehill

It is quiet and peaceful today, but in autumn 1642 this was a very noisy and dangerous place. The first battle of the English Civil War took place here at Edgehill on Sunday October 23rd.

All attempts to reconcile King Charles I and the Parliamentarian factions in the country had irretrievably broken down. Both sides began raising armies to enforce their own particular desires and war was rapidly becoming inevitable.

During the autumn of 1642 King Charles I had based himself in Shrewsbury. The King was becoming restless just hanging around the Welsh borders and decided that it was the most appropriate moment to gather his forces and march on London. At almost the same time the Roundheads decided that they too needed to establish their superiority and so they marched towards the Royalist army to force a battle.

On Saturday 22nd October both armies began to realise that they were becoming very close to each other. The Royalists were occupying the higher ground surrounding the villages of Ratley, Warmington and Farnborough while the Parliamentarians were encamped near to Kineton which was situated on the plain below.

The Royalists decided that they held the advantage and would force an engagement. Early in the morning of the 23rd October King Charles' army marched down the steep escarpment of Edge Hill to do battle with his enemies.

Generally speaking there was no great difference between the strengths of the two opposing armies. The Parliamentarian forces were led by the Earl of Essex and had a slight superiority in numbers with 15,000 men compared to the Royalists who had gathered together slightly fewer at 12,400. However, the Roundhead superiority was only to be found in the quantity of foot soldiers. Cavalries were a more lethal fighting force and both were equally matched with about 2,500 mounted warriors each.

Many of the foot soldiers on both sides were inexperienced and poorly trained. Often they possessed little in the way of efficient weapons, mostly relying on various types of pike staffs. In some cases all they had to fight with were basic agricultural implements that they had brought with them. Artillery was in short supply on both sides. The Royalists only possessed sixteen guns in total while the Roundheads could muster just a pitiful seven.

Prince Rupert of the Rhine gave the order for the Royalists to attack and they were initially successful in gaining the upper hand. Then things started to go wrong for them. When sections of the King's army reached the Roundhead supply train in Kineton they abandoned their official duties and found more personal gains by plundering the Parliamentarian baggage.

The Parliamentarians had their share of success as well. They managed to push the Royalist centre backwards, and at one time succeeded in capturing the Royal Standard through the efforts of Ensign Arthur Young. The standard was eventually regained by Captain John Smith who bravely chased through the Roundhead ranks in order to retrieve it. The Parliamentarians proved to be no more disciplined than their opponents, for they also broke ranks to take part in looting whenever the opportunity presented itself.

When the armies drew apart towards the end of the day both sides had suffered similar losses of approximately 500 killed and 1500 wounded. The two rival forces held their respective positions overnight, but on the following morning the Earl of Essex took the decision to retreat to the safety of Warwick castle several miles to the north.

King Charles I opted to continue to London, but made a slight diversion to take the opportunity to capture the Roundhead garrison at Banbury on the way. The Earl of Essex took his men from Warwick straight to London reaching the city before the King. This enabled him to recruit more men to deter the Royalists from entering the capital. Charles realised that he had little option but to abandon all hope of recapturing London and withdrew his forces to Oxford which became established as the Royalist headquarters for the rest of the war.

So, with both sides unwilling to continue fighting to the end, the Battle of Edgehill could be considered to be a "score draw". The indecisive outcome of the confrontation and the well-matched balance of the opposing forces in the aftermath prevented either side from establishing a clear advantage. This equilibrium was a major factor in the war becoming drawn out over the next four years until Oliver Cromwell was finally able to establish the superiority of his new Parliament.

Sunrising Hill

Sunrising Hill provides excellent panoramic views over the Warwickshire Plain. Looking out over the scarp edge the southern parts of Warwickshire are a mixture of bright yellow and a variety of shades of green. In the far distance the Malvern Hills form a grey, lumpy horizon.

I am overlooking the countryside so beloved by the great William Shakespeare. Through the centre of the plain the River Avon gains in strength as it gathers up its tributaries on the journey to join the mighty River Severn at Tewkesbury. The fertile farmland gave wealth to the region, leading to small, prosperous towns and villages, none more than Stratford-upon-Avon, home of the Bard himself. Stratford can clearly be seen from Sunrising, occupying the centre-stage of the plain.

To the north west is the Forest of Arden. While the woodland is not as dense as it would have been in Shakespeare's days the area is still noted for its oak trees, small woodlands and hedgerows.

On the plain immediately below the escarpment is where the Battle of Edgehill took place and there are two information boards on the hill that show the positions of the rival forces as they struggled for the domination of England.

Upton House

Just half a mile away from the top of Sunrising Hill is Upton House. This National Trust property is well worth taking a look at by making a short diversion. The front of the house can be viewed from the road, but it is the contents of the house that are the principal attraction.

The beauty of Upton House is in its capacity as an art gallery. The house was purchased in 1927 by the 2nd Earl of Bearsted to house his impressive art collection. The Earl owed his vast wealth to his inheritance from his father, who was the founder of the oil company "Shell".

There are many fine paintings on display at Upton House. I will just mention three here that are particularly worthy of note. "Adoration of Kings" a triptych painted by Hieronymus Bosch in 1495, "The Labourers" (1779) by William Stubbs, and "Bacino di San Marco" (1725), a masterpiece view of Venice by the celebrated Canaletto.

An extensive range of porcelain is also exhibited. There are fine examples of Rococo, Derby, Bow, Derby and a selection of Sevres pottery from France.

The current house dates from 1695 but it has been extended on several occasions since then. The construction is of local yellow sandstone. The interior decoration is very much in the "Art Deco" style popular during the 1930's.

The gardens have been extensively redeveloped to represent how they would have appeared in the 1930's. The main feature is a sweeping lawn, with herbaceous borders and terraces leading down to an ornamental lake. Former fishponds have been developed into a "bog garden". The Upton House Gardens include a magnificent collection of asters. The gardens are also home to a wide selection of wildlife, with birds, butterflies and insects visible wherever you look.

Alkerton, Shennington and Epwell

From Sunrising Hill the Macmillan Way swings away from the escarpment and heads over open fields. Just before reaching Alkerton the path joins the D'Arcy Dalton Way and the two will remain joined until I reach Epwell.

The D'Arcy Dalton Way is named in memory of Colonel D'Arcy Dalton who campaigned for more than 50 years to preserve rights of way throughout Oxfordshire. Starting by the Oxford Canal at Wormleighton the path links the Oxford Canal, Oxfordshire Way, Thames Path and The Ridgeway. The path finishes where it joins the Ridgeway at Wayland Smithy, an ancient Neolithic long barrow near to Ashbury on the Berkshire Downs. It is 65 miles long and was designated by the Oxfordshire Fieldpaths Society to celebrate its Diamond Jubilee in 1986. Colonel D'Arcy Dalton was one of the society's founding members.

The path skirts the small village of Alkerton, which has a fine example of a medieval church. One of the bells is believed to date back to 1400. St Michael's Church dates from the 12th century and is just visible to my left.

The houses in the larger village of Shennington are mostly constructed from the local ironstone with thatched roofs. There is a large village green in the centre.

The path continues over open fields, threading between the tops of Epwell Hill and Yarn Hill. The compact village of Epwell sits in a hollow between the hills. Epwell is a pretty little village and provides a satisfying ending to today's walk.

Most of today has been spent steadily flirting with the northern edge of the Cotswolds. Tomorrow I will be advancing into the more well known areas of one of the most beautiful regions of England.

EPWELL TO STOW ON THE WOLD

DAY 10

15 MILES

Ditchedge Lane

The weather has definitely changed for the better and for the first time on this expedition I am able to display the bright green MacMillan tee shirt provided by the charity to publicise my efforts.

I have to take great care to follow the correct path out of Epwell. There are several footpaths spreading out from the church and I need to be sure to take the correct one. The D'Arcy Dalton Way takes its own route from here.

A short climb past the church at Epwell takes me to a carved wooden gate. The single gate has carvings on either post, depicting a kingfisher, dragonfly and frog on the left hand side, with a songbird and flower on the right. The inscription reads "In Memory of Mary Dale December 1955 to August 2007".

The path from here is easily marked by a radio mast on the hill and I soon reach it. I am rewarded with a wonderfully clear view across the Stour Valley. From the radio mast my route travels almost due south in a straight line following a good track. This is a green road known as Ditchedge Lane and marks the boundary between Oxfordshire and Warwickshire. Ditchedge Lane was probably an early Saxon trade route although there is a possibility that it may be even older. One thing seems to be absent. As far as I can see there is just one minor glitch in that there does not appear to be a ditch here for the lane to be on the edge of. Still, I can't have everything. The terrific views provided from the track will be with me for the next two miles and it is a fine start to the day.

Traitor's Ford

Ditchedge Lane joins the Traitor's Ford Lane at Traitor's Ford. The crossing is situated in a pleasant wooded area with the infant stream covering the road by just a few inches.

Quite why this shallow ford across the River Stour is so named is somewhat in dispute. Some say that it was not originally Traitor's Ford at all, but Trader's Ford from the trade route that I have just been following. There are other stories that a traitor was hanged at this point during the civil war.

A notice at the ford gives a different spin on things.

As we have already seen there was a great deal of activity in these parts in the very early days of the English Civil War. The Royalists harassed the locals for food and horses together with anything else that could be used to supply the requirements of the King's army. No doubt there was not an accurate inventory of items taken and many were kept for personal uses. Understandably this did not make the Royalists very popular with the local people.

In particular there was a Colonel Gerard Croker who lived in nearby Hook Norton. Croker was a member of the King's Oxford Horse Cavalry and an enthusiastic scavenger of supplies for the army at Edgehill. Many atrocities were reportedly committed by Croker and his men as they raided their neighbours for their goods. They were despised for their actions and considered to be traitors to the people.

Local legend has it that the tormented souls of Croker's victims haunt the area around the ford. On dark nights ghosts of white horses that were taken by the marauders can be seen, and the anguished cries of their victims fill the air.

Whichford

Whichford is a nice little village that sits under the scarp face of the Cotswolds. I am somewhat surprised to be confronted with a life-sized statue of a knight in shining armour astride his white charger. The knight is pointing his lance menacingly forward, ready for combat. Fortunately this was not some kind of surreal guardian barring my progress, but a novel way of presenting the local inn, "The Norman Knight". The inn is festooned with union flags, no doubt in preparation for the forthcoming Queen's Jubilee celebrations.

I would have appreciated the assistance of the knight to give me a ride up the face of Whichford Hill. I was puffing a bit by the time that I reached the top of the woodland that occupies much of the south east side. The Macmillan Way takes a semicircular route around the wood before dropping down into the village of Long Compton.

Long Compton and The Rollright Stones

Long Compton is the last village that I will pass through before leaving Warwickshire. As its name suggests the community is a long ribbon of about a mile in length. The village is home to 750 people. The most interesting thing that I discovered about Long Compton is that it allegedly has a centuries old tradition of witchcraft.

The reputation goes back at least to Tudor times, and is probably in some way connected with the nearby Rollright Stones.

The story I uncovered is a tragedy that occurred a little under 150 years ago. In 1875 James Heywood appointed himself as the local vigilante and launched a one man campaign against the local witches. My sense of humour instantly conjures up an image of Charles Bronson playing the part in a Michael Winner film version called "Death Witch". Heywood murdered his neighbour, 80 years old Anne Tennant, whom he claimed had bewitched him under her evil spells. The unfortunate lady had toads in her garden which in Heywood's warped view was sufficient evidence of witchcraft to justify imposing his own savage penalty on her.

The deluded Heywood readily admitted to his crime and in court claimed that there were another sixteen witches residing in the village and that it was his duty to kill them all. In full Monty Python manner he suggested that Anne Tennant's body should be weighed against the Holy Bible to prove beyond question that she was a witch.

The judge at the trial declared Heywood to be insane and ordered him to be imprisoned at Warwick. During his confinement Heywood continued to claim that he had been put under an evil spell and refused to take food and drink to enforce his protests. Inevitably he perished through malnutrition.

As I make my way through Long Compton I am particularly careful not to upset any old ladies. Just in case. To be absolutely certain I keep a sharp look-out for black cats and toads as well.

The Rollright Stones

The Rollright Stones are slightly off the main route of the Macmillan Way but provide an interesting diversion. In a similar manner to many other ancient monuments the megaliths sit on a hill top overlooking the lands below. From the great efforts that must have been made during their construction these stones must have held a position of great importance in the minds of our ancestors. Until somebody invents a real working tardis it is unlikely that we will ever discover exactly what that importance was. This sense of the unknown and the air of mystery is one of the great fascinations about all of these types of ancient locations.

The name of the area, "Rollright" originates from "Hrolla Landriht" meaning Land of Hrolla. There are three distinct sets of stones and as is common throughout the country there is a local legend attached to them as well as the prehistorical significance.

The main group of stones dates from the Neolithic Period of around 2,500 BC and is known as the King's Men. There are 77 stones formed in a circle measuring approximately thirty yards in diameter. The stones vary in height and shape and are made of oolitic limestone. The stones have all suffered from heavy weathering over the years and are deeply pitted. Mosses and lichens have made the limestone their homes and some of the lichen formations are believed to be many centuries old.

Across the road, but still only fifty yards away from the King's Men, stands a solitary stone, larger than all of the others. It has a curious shape that has been likened to that of a seal balancing a ball on its nose. It is not only the weather that has shaped this stone, man has also played his part. The stone was believed to have protective powers and passersby allegedly used to chip a piece away and carry it in their pocket for good luck. There was believed to be a sharp increase in this vandalism during the Civil War when the Royalist forces were in the area, because the soldiers believed that carrying a piece of this stone would protect them from injury during battle.

The third group of stones are about 400 yards away to the east of the main ring. They are known as the Whispering Knights and have occupied this position for about 5,000 years. They are part of an ancient Neolithic burial chamber known as a dolmen. There are five stones in this group, which are leaning towards each other. The name "Whispering Knights" comes from the conspiratorial manner in which they are huddled together, as if they are attempting to conceal a secret.

Now we have the stones in our minds, let us look at the local legend. In fact there are several legends, but let us study the main one first.

Long, long ago a highly ambitious king, accompanied by his entourage, was passing through Rollright when they came across an old woman. This woman gave the king a prophesy, "Seven long strides shall thou take and if Long Compton thou canst see, King of all England thou shalt be".

The king, knowing that Long Compton was on the plain below strode off to confirm that even more power and fortune would be his for the taking and announcing, "Stick, stock, stone, as King of England I shall be known". However his arrogance was short-lived for on taking his seventh and final stride the village of Long Compton became hidden behind a rise in the ground known as the Arch Druid's Barrow. The king turned to glare angrily at the woman. The old crone cackled (as they do) "As Long Compton thou canst not see, King of England thou shalt not be. Rise up stick and stand still stone for King of England thou shalt be none. Thou and thy men hoar stones shall be, and I myself an eldern tree".

At this the King was immediately transformed to stone where he stood and his men, who were sitting in a large circular group, were also turned to stone. A group of knights who were whispering nearby (probably wondering what the king was doing with this woman because everyone knows that no good ever comes from these incidents) were also turned to stone. The old woman turned into an eldern tree, presumably to keep watch over her charges and gloat for all eternity.

Local legend tells that the king and his men come back to life at midnight and dance in their circle before descending to the nearby stream for a drink. Anyone who witnesses this event is reputed to be driven mad. I would imagine it is more likely that anyone claiming to have seen such a thing would have taken rather too much of the prize-winning local Hook Norton ale!

The story was first recorded in the late 16th century and probably originated in the century before. This was a time when the church was trying to discourage people from going near ancient pagan sites and the clergy were not above spreading such tales to enforce their commands.

Almost inevitably there are also stories that the stones cannot be counted because the devil moves them (or the effect of the ale is kicking in). One version has it that if you count the same number three times you will die, while a contrary version states that if you arrive at the same total three times in succession your heart's desire will be fulfilled. Allegedly an inspired local baker tried to count the stones by placing a bread roll on each one. However each time he finished some of the rolls had gone missing. The baker claimed it was either the devil or the fairies that took them. On the other hand I know lots of people who if somebody tried that sort of thing would find it absolutely hilarious to nip out from behind a tree and swipe a couple of rolls when the baker's back was turned.

Whatever the stories are behind the Rollright Stones it provides both a peaceful and mystical place. It is a place to sit and wonder. What possessed our forebears to create these formations and what did the people hope to achieve from their efforts? Rollright Stones provide a great location for a picnic, but be careful where you put your bread rolls.

Chastleton House

Following the Macmillan Way along the scarp edge is a wonderful afternoon stroll. There are exceptional views from this ridge across the Gloucestershire Cotswolds to my right. The track flattens out after the A44 and takes me through a parkland estate to Chastleton House.

Chastleton is a Stuart manor house that has been carefully preserved by the National Trust. Notice that I say preserved and not restored. This is because this house is a bit different. Everything has been done to preserve the house as it was and not restore to an "as new" pristine appearance.

The house is open to the public but the hours are restricted to Wednesday to Saturday afternoons only. (Correct at the time of writing in 2012).

The first view of Chastleton House is through the arched stone gateway. Constructed of Cotswold stone the three-storey house sits only a short way back from the road. The front elevation is topped by five gables.

The house was built between 1607 and 1612 for Walter Jones who came from a wealthy family of wool merchants.

Very little was changed at the house until 1991 when it was purchased by the National Trust. The house had obviously suffered the inevitable ravages that time brings to everything, but the Trust were determined to do something different with Chastleton House and great efforts were made to preserve the contents as they were.

The most impressive room is the Long Gallery. This room with its barrel vaulted ceiling is 22metres (72ft) in length and is a unique example of Jacobean design. Also not to be missed is the Great Chamber which is based on a Renaissance theme. The panelling features classically inspired themes and the friezes include representations of the Twelve Prophets of the Old Testament. Another room of note is the kitchen where the visitor can see many items used by the workers who spent most of their day "below stairs".

Outside there are examples of Jacobean topiary, and a vegetable garden. The lawn to the north of the house was once used for croquet and has a special significance. Walter Whitmore-Jones who owned Chastleton House during the mid-nineteenth century wrote the first "Rules of Croquet" which were published in "The Field" magazine in 1865. Chastleton House can therefore lay claim to the game of croquet being formalised on its lawns.

The last feature of note at Chastleton House is the fine dovecote situated in the field on the opposite side of the lane. This feature was built to be visible from the house. Sited half-way up the hillside it makes a striking picture.

Adlestrop

The first thing that I see as I come to Adlestrop is a wooden bus shelter. This is no ordinary bus shelter. Across the whole width of the back of the shelter is a giant sign announcing "Adlestrop" in large white letters painted on a brown background.

The sign is from the village railway station that was closed in 1966. Adlestrop Station became immortalised in the poem by Edward Thomas (1878-1917). The rhyme tells of the time that Thomas was a passenger on a train from Oxford to Worcester that was forced to make an unscheduled stop at Adlestrop. Nothing significant happened as Edward Thomas sat in the carriage waiting for the train to move on. From the restrictions of his compartment Thomas could only see the name of the station to one side, trees and grasses on the other, and listen to the songs of the birds.

Yes, I remember Adlestrop –
The name because one afternoon
Of heat the express-train drew up there
Unwontedly. It was late June.

The steam hissed. Someone cleared his throat.
No one left and no one came
On the bare platform. What I saw
Was Adlestrop – only the name

And willows, willow-herb, and grass,
And meadowsweet, and haycocks dry,
No whit less still and lonely fair
Than the high cloudlets in the sky.

And for that minute a blackbird sang
Close by, and round him, mistier,
Farther and farther, all the birds
Of Oxfordshire and Gloucestershire.

As I leave Adlestrop I cross a road bridge over the railway line. The former station building has been converted into a private residence, but the sign lives on. In a bus stop.

The Oddingtons

The villages of Lower and Upper Oddington are typical of the many attractive Cotswold villages. Every house is meticulously kept. It occurs to me as I pass through them that there is not a single for sale board on any of the houses. No doubt once people settle in places like these they are very reticent to leave.

St. Nicholas's Parish Church at Lower Oddington has an interesting interior with a restored painting of "The Doom" on the north wall of the nave. The original painting dates from the 15ᵗʰ century.

Stow on the Wold

The Macmillan Way skips around the south side of Stow on the Wold through the village of Maugersbury. It is a distance of only half a mile into the town from the village so there seems no point in not having a look while I am here.

Stow on the Wold is the highest town in the Cotswolds. Standing on the top of a 700ft (230m) hill the town overlooks the north Cotswolds. Stow does not have the best reputation for weather although it is nice and fine today. It has been known to snow here in May and June, and the wind can be very sharp and harsh. Not for nothing do the houses appear to be huddled together for warmth.

There is even a local ditty that runs "At Stow on the Wold, the wind blows cold".

Some of the buildings at Stow on the Wold date back to the 16th century and they all have that welcoming warm honey glow of Cotswold stone. The Royalist Hotel in Digbeth Street lays a claim to being the oldest established inn in England. There has been an inn on the site since 947 AD.

There has been a settlement here since the Iron Age. In the same manner as Stamford, where I passed through a week ago, the town grew because of the needs of travellers. In Stamford's case it was the bridge over the Welland, but in this case it was because every road through the north Cotswolds passed through Stow. The ancient Cotswold Ridgeway and Saltway crossed here, which led to an Iron Age fort being developed from around 700BC. Moving onwards the Roman Fosse Way also passed through Stow, where it was joined by six other roads making this a very important crossing. With so many roads converging on the same place it provided an excellent opportunity for traders. Added to all of this there was plentiful supply of water from underground springs, so it was a perfect place to develop a settlement.

The first charter for a weekly market was granted by King Henry I in 1107. This was followed by Edward III who added a seven day fair held in August. In 1476 Edward IV changed this to two five-day fairs to be held in May and October. That pretty well remains the case today, except that the two five day fairs have evolved into horse fairs where thousands of Romany's descend on the town to trade their animals and meet with family and friends.

There are several narrow alleys leading into the Market Square. The alleys are known as "tures" or "chures" and were used to drive sheep to the market through a restricted space so that they could be counted. At the peak of the Cotswold wool industry it was not uncommon for up to 20,000 sheep to be traded during a single day.

This brings us to the question of how did the shepherds count sheep before the advent of mechanical click counters and computerisation?

Our ancestors used a rhyme developed from the ancient Brythonic Celtic language generally referred to as Yahn, Tain, Tethera.

The system is based on the number 20. This is a far more practical number base to work in when counting large numbers than decimal or dozens. Each time the number 20 was reached the shepherd would jut out another finger or place a stick or stone on the ground. By only using his fingers he could count up to 200. Across the country there are slight variations on the pronunciations and names but the principle remains the same. For example in the Yorkshire Dales Pip replaces Mumph to represent a quantity of five. There are numerous other small variations around the country but the basic principal remains the same.

It is a shame not to put it to the test, so I will attempt to count the people that come by in traditional Cotswold fashion. Fingers at the ready........here I go!

Yahn, Tain, Tethera, Methera, Mumph,

Hither, Lither, Auver, Dauver, Dic,

Yahndic, Taindic, Tetherdic, Metherdic, Mumphit,

Yahnmumphit, Tainmumphit, Tethermumphit, Methermumfit, Jigit

And that is all there is to it!

Battle of Stow on the Wold

Stow on the Wold was the setting for the last battle of the First Civil War. The English Civil War was not a single series of battles as many people tend to assume, but a mixture of battles, skirmishes and raids that can be divided into three distinct sets. The First Civil War (1642 to 1646) was fought between the Parliamentarian and Royalist armies. The Second Civil War (1648 to 1649) pitted the supporters of Charles I against the Long Parliament. The Third Civil War was contested by the supporters of Charles II and the Rump Parliament. The combined series ended with the Battle of Worcester on 3rd September 1651.

Let us return to the days of the First Civil War. Yesterday we learned that the opening battle at Edgehill was indecisive and we left off where King Charles I had set up his Royalist headquarters in Oxford and the Parliamentarians had established a stronghold in London. During the subsequent four years both armies criss-crossed the country, chasing each other and trying to force battles when they were the stronger, then running away when they thought that their opponents had the upper hand. With Stow on the Wold being situated at the junction of eight roads they were forever chasing each other through this locality. Just add the music and it must have been just like a Benny Hill sketch!

Inevitably with all of this to-ing and fro-ing there was bound to be some point when they would both end up in Stow on the Wold at the same time. This is exactly what happened on September 21st 1646. Following his defeat at the Battle of Naseby, King Charles knew that his only chance of continuing the campaign was to regroup at Oxford . He charged Sir Jacob Astley with gathering up the remnants of his army and mustering them at Oxford. The Parliamentarians soon got to hear of this and, led by Colonel Thomas Morgan, the Roundhead army attempted to block the Cavaliers progress.

Eventually they met about a mile and a half to the north of Stow on the Wold on March 23rd. The Royalist forces were routed and many fled to seek safety in the town itself. The Roundheads followed in pursuit and there was literally "blood on the streets". By late afternoon it was all over. Sir Jacob Astley was captured and many soldiers were taken prisoner. King Charles managed to sneak out of Oxford in disguise and eventually surrendered to the Parliamentarians at Newark. The First Civil War had ended.

My day has also ended at Stow on the Wold. I am just a smidgen short of halfway after covering 144 miles. Tomorrow will take me through some of the prettiest villages in the Cotswolds. I can't wait.

STOW ON THE WOLD TO RENDCOMB

DAY 11
17 MILES

Lower Slaughter

Today's exertions will take me through some of the most delightful villages in the Cotswolds.

The route from Stow on the Wold follows the busy A429 southwards out of the town. It follows the course of the old Roman road, "The Fosse Way". This road was constructed by the Romans shortly after their invasion of AD43 and covered the 182 miles between Lincoln (Lindum Colonia) and Exeter (Isca Dumnoniorum). The name was derived from the Latin word "fossa" meaning a ditch. In the early years of the Roman occupation the Fosse Way also marked the western edge of the colonisation, so there could possibly have been a marker ditch alongside the road. For much of its course the Macmillan Way has run parallel with this old road and will continue to do so for the next couple of days. Quite amazingly my route only crosses this ancient route twice, here at Stow and again at Castle Combe in a couple of days time.

At the foot of the hill the Macmillan Way takes its leave of the former Roman highway and sets off on a pleasant course across the fields. The tiny River Dickler flows through these fields on its way to join the River Eye just above Bourton-on-the Water. Although tiny the river must possess some reasonable force or there would not have been a mill built on its banks where my path crossed over the stream. Hyde Mill is highly significant for another reason. It marks the half-way point of the MacMillan Way. As I cross the footbridge over the river my mind shifts to recognise that I am now playing the second half.

Lower Slaughter sounds as though it took its name from the grisly horrors of a battlefield. In fact the name has its origins in the Domesday Book as "Sclostre", meaning wetland or slough.

Lower Slaughter is one of the prettiest villages in England. I am very fortunate to be here in the early morning of a quiet mid-week day. There is hardly anybody else about to spoil my enjoyment of this marvellous little village. I can only imagine what it is like on a sunny summer Sunday afternoon.

The River Eye takes centre stage, literally forming the centrepiece of the main road. Small stone footbridges cross the sparkling waterway as it makes its way sedately through the village. On either side of the stream the Cotswold stone cottages give off their warm welcoming glow. Most of the dwellings boast mullioned windows and some have projecting gabled roofs. The 13th century church of St.Mary the Virgin sits behind a stone wall, guarded by yew trees and a splendid old lych gate.

Opposite the church stands the "Slaughters Country Inn" which looks as though it would make a wonderful location for a romantic weekend in the country.

At the western end of the village is the Mill Museum. The mill is in contrast to the rest of the village being constructed from red brick. The museum is open to the public and also offers a welcoming tea room.

Lower Slaughter is one of those places where you just want to sit and lose yourself in the surroundings. There are plenty of seats to accommodate this. A glance at my watch shows that I have spent far longer here than I had originally anticipated. I must hurry off to keep to the day's schedule but I will definitely be back here on a future occasion.

River Windrush

There is a short uphill stretch out of Lower Slaughter taking me over the ridge and down into the Windrush valley.

The River Windrush is one of several waters that run south from the Cotswold Hills into the River Thames. Rising in the hills near to Taddington the Windrush flows for 40 miles before making its contribution to the River Thames at Newbridge.

On its way to boost the majestic royalty of the river Thames the Windrush contributes its own beauty to the places along its banks, most notably in the towns of Bourton-on-the-Water, Burford and Witney.

The waters of the Windrush also have a special quality that was responsible for the fame of Witney in the production of blankets. The river passes over geological areas which result in a perfect mixture of sulphates and nitrates in the water. When the blankets were finished by washing in the water it gave them gave them a unique whiteness. This resulted in Witney blankets being much in demand from the 17th century onwards. Yes folks, before the days of modern soap powders people could tell that "Windrush washes whiter"!

Cold Aston

Old Blue Eyes sang "New York, New York, so good they named it twice."

They named Cold Aston twice as well. The sign at the entrance to the village proclaims "Cold Aston (Aston Blank)".

Back in the days of the ever reliable Domesday Book of 1086 the village was simple known as Estone, probably derived from the Saxon "Est Tun" meaning eastern farmstead.

From the 13th century the name became Cold Aston and remained so for some 300 years. During the 16th century the name was changed to Aston Blank. This was not derived from a corny 1970's quiz show where people could add their own selection to win a cheque book and pen, but a name allegedly derived from the French "blanc", meaning white or bare. The new name was not at all popular with the locals who campaigned for the name to be changed back again. They got their wish in the end but it was not until some 400 years later in 1972 that the former title of Cold Aston was officially restored. Who said that local democracy is slow to give results? Power to the people!

The village green has a wonderful sycamore tree that simply demands admiration. If truth be told I was more interested in the village pub opposite. Today was the first really warm day of the entire walk and I had been looking forward to a refreshing "livener" all the way from Lower Slaughter. The best laid plans of mice and men went swiftly aglay as I noticed the contractor's boards outside and huge holes where the door and windows should have been. Not yet another country pub closing to become another converted period house? A quick read of the board was reassuring; the Plough will be open again next year after an extensive refurbishment.

Bangup Lane

The route out of Cold Aston follows a track with the intriguing title of "Bangup Lane". Make up your own jokes. Moving swiftly on........

Turkdean, Hampnett and Yanworth

The next three villages each have a different character.

Turkdean is a small village with a small green and a church. The houses are mainly spread along the roadside. The Macmillan Way uses a sunken footpath to take a short-cut downhill to the few buildings of Lower Dean. The path is steep with overhanging trees and is still a little slippery from the spring rains.

After risking life and limb crossing the busy A40 I wander into Hampnett. This small village provides some wonderful views of the surrounding countryside. I drop down a side road to a row of cottages, crossing a small stone bridge on the way. This bridge crosses the infant River Leach which has its source just a few fields away. The sparkling clear water will run for another 18 miles before entering the River Thames a little downstream of Lechlade. The bridge parapet is a lovely place to just sit and watch the small stream for a while, with the stone cottages and slopes of the hills in the background.

I enter the village of Yanworth via a farmyard which featured an impressive set of barn buildings. These barns look better looked-after than many of the houses in some other places. The nearby church also looks in magnificent condition. Some of the structure dates from Norman times. I ventured inside to view the wall painting of Old Father Time. This is a somewhat unusual subject for a work of art in a church. It makes a change from the usual Renaissance type of religious paintings.

Yanworth is very much an estate village with the characteristic uniformity of green painted woodwork adorning most of the houses. The village is immaculately maintained by the residents. Walking through the village I can see many delightful Cotswold cottages enhanced by a wide range of window-boxes and hanging baskets all in full bloom. The front lawns were all perfectly manicured with exquisite floral borders. It was difficult to find a favourite to photograph so I ended up taking quite a few different snaps of several properties. If the village has a "Best Garden" competition it would be almost impossible to judge.

From Yanworth Mill the route follows the River Coln for a little over one mile. There is a track which provides easy walking. This is a very relaxing section with wooded slopes rising to my left and the River Coln flowing through water meadows to my right. Pheasants strut around without an apparent care in the world. The trees are providing a cool shade to walk under. Isn't life wonderful?

Chedworth Roman Villa

Chedworth Roman Villa is one of the largest examples of its type in Britain. The villa is located in a sheltered position overlooking the River Coln. It is near to the Fosse Way and only 8 miles from the old Roman city of Cirencester. In those days the city was known by the Romans as Corinium Dobunnorum.

The remains of the villa were discovered in 1864 by gamekeeper Thomas Margetts. He was digging out a ferret when he found remains of paving and pottery. The site was then excavated over the following two years by the amateur archaeologist James Farrer (1812 – 1879).

Farrer found many artefacts but the most significant discovery was a series of mosaic floors. The floors gave the find a great significance and encouraged historians to make further explorations. More work followed, with the owner of the land, the Earl of Eldon, financing the cost of the archaeological digs. The Earl also paid for protective coverings for the mosaics and the construction of a mock-Tudor house in which the excavated treasurers could be stored and displayed. In 1924 the site was purchased by the National Trust.

The construction of the villa was believed to be in 120AD and the first phase consisted of housing in the south and west of the site, with a small bath house in the north.

The second phase of the development took place towards the end of the 3rd century when the houses were enlarged and the bath house considerably expanded. The third and final phase saw the villa transformed into a stately dwelling. The buildings were extended to form a central courtyard and another bath house was added.

The development by the National Trust has gradually turned Chedworth into arguably the best site for learning about the Roman way of life in Britain. I was able to watch an absorbing introductory video that highlighted the excavations and the way the Romans lived. Interactive study is actively encouraged here with rooms set aside for dressing up as wealthy Romans, servants or legionnaires. Chedworth is very popular with schools so if you visit during the week in term-time come prepared to be surrounded by enthusiastic mini-centurions!

In total the length of discovered walls add up to over a mile, but when you have seen one villa wall you have seen them all. What many people really come to see at Chedworth are the excavated mosaic floors. These were put under a special protective viewing cover in 2011. Special raised walkways take the visitor over the mosaics, enabling closer inspection of the patterns from immediately above.

There is little doubt that Chedworth must have been owned by a very wealthy Roman family. It seems that Gloucestershire was a preferred location for the well-off even in those days. Sometimes it seems nothing has changed on that score for nearly two thousand years!

Rendcomb

Walking across the fields on my way towards Rendcomb I am spending more time watching the sky than I am the surrounding hills. Specifically I am looking out for biplanes. Just across the fields is a restored World War One airfield known as RFC Rendcomb. It is privately owned and is the home of the Aero Super Batics display team.

The team flies orange coloured Boeing Stearman biplanes, first produced in 1933. They were originally designed as a training plane and many of the World War Two pilots received their first instructions in these aircraft. These biplanes are a little bit different to those originals. They are supercharged with 450 horsepower radial engines instead of the original 220 horsepower, and the fuselage is steel tube and plastic covering, rather than wooden struts and varnished fabric.

All of the controls are in the rear cockpit from where the pilot flies the plane. The front cockpit is clear. This is because – and you have to believe this – during the aerobatic display a young lady will climb out of that front cockpit, climb onto the top wing and perform acrobatics. At the same time the planes will be looping, rolling and even flying upside down! The planes will reach speeds of 150mph and at times will be pulling up to 4G.

Wingwalking started in 1918 when a young American by the name of Ormer Locklear had a technical problem during a flight. Whereas any normal, sane person would have landed the plane to sort things out, young Ormer simply climbed out of the cockpit, wandered along the wing, fixed the problem then strolled back to complete the flight. All in mid-air! After the war he entertained crowds at air shows by walking between two airplanes. Since then there has been some added safety but it is still an incredible thing to do.

What is more, anyone can do it. All you have to do is go to www.aerosuperbatics.com and fill out a form, pay £399 (as of November 2012) and you can be a wingwalker too. A day training and a flight to show off what you have learned. Any takers?

What me? You must be kidding. I will happily walk these 290 miles to Chesil Beach but 10 foot along a biplane wing seems far too far to me; about 10 feet too far to be precise.

The small village of Rendcomb is the end of the walk for today. The village is dominated by the Italianate buildings of Rendcomb Court, now part of the Rendcomb College, a large day and boarding school. No doubt the school can boast great achievements, but as far as Rendcomb is concerned I have seen where the real high-flyers are.

DIVERSION TO CIRENCESTER

9.5 MILES

There is an alternative route from Rendcomb and for the completeness of the book I returned some weeks later to undertake this additional section. Instead of passing through the grounds of Cirencester Park and the delightful Hailey Wood the alternative route follows the River Churn southwards to the old Roman town of Cirencester and then turns westwards to rejoin the main MacMillan Way at the Tunnel House Inn.

North Cerney

The first village that I come to on the diversion is North Cerney.

There has been a village here since well before the Norman conquest. There is a record of the King of Mercia granting land here to a man by the name of Alfeah in 852AD. The Domesday Book refers to the settlement as Cernai.

The Bathurst Arms is a splendid country inn with gardens extending to the banks of the River Churn. I love the dense green ivy covering the front of the inn.

Baunton

Two miles further down the River Churn I arrive at Baunton. This is another old village that can trace its history back to before the Norman Invasion. The village is only half the size of North Cerney having a population of approximately 300 people. There are several grade II listed buildings in Baunton, including the 16th century manor house.

The Church of St. Mary Magdalene was built in 1150 by the Augustinian Monks from Cirencester Abbey. This church is well worth popping into to view the large painting of St.Christopher. The scene depicts St.Christopher carrying the childhood Christ across a stream.

Cirencester

It may not seem like it now, but in its Roman days Cirencester was England's second largest city. In those days it was known as Corinium Dobunnum, or simply Corinium. Today the population is a comparatively modest 19,000 but in perspective that still makes Cirencester the largest town in the Cotswolds.

Before the Romans arrived the area was the major settlement of the Dobunni tribe. The Dobunnians were a peaceful Celtic tribe who spread themselves across the area we would recognise as Somerset, Avon, Bristol, Gloucestershire and Wiltshire. They were primarily a farming and crafts community and had little enthusiasm for warfare. When the Romans came to settle in AD43 the Dobunni readily submitted to the Roman ways and were one of the very first of the British tribes to become integrated into the Roman Empire.

One interesting thing that I discovered during my researches was that the Dobunni were one of very few tribes that minted their own form of coins prior to the Roman invasion.

The Roman fort of Corinium was originally a frontier post on the western edge of the Roman Empire. It guarded the place where a crossing point was required to carry the Fosse Way over the River Churn. At this time the Dobunni settlement was about five miles to the north. The Romans invited the Celts to move to the safer area surrounding the fort and renamed it Corinium Dobunnum. At one time the enclosed town occupied 24 acres (1 square km).

In 70AD the border was pushed out as far as Wales and Corinium became more important as a junction of three major routes. It is still an important road junction today with an extensive ring road system being necessary to help keep the town centre clear of traffic.

Artefacts from the Roman occupation can be seen at the award-winning Corinium Museum. No visit to Cirencester would be complete without a tour of this collection. The museum is situated in Park Street and is open throughout the year. There is a superb collection of mosaics housed in the museum.

The remains of the Roman Amphitheatre can still be seen at Cirencester just to the south of the ring road. Most of the earthworks are in their original location and I am able to walk across the grounds and imagine what it must have been like as an ancient centre of entertainment. There is some evidence that the Saxons used the amphitheatre as a fortress during the 5th and 6th centuries.

After the decline of the Roman Empire this area of southern England was regularly fought over. Initially the Saxons took control. It was the Saxons who gave the town the name its present name was derived from, Cerne Cester , the castle by the Cerne. Later Cirencester was taken over by the Hwicce who were a sub-Kingdom of Mercia.

Everything changed with the arrival of the Normans. Straight after the conquest the town was given to the Earl of Hereford but in 1075 had reverted back to the crown.

In 1117 Cirencester was placed under the control of Cirencester Abbey. This sparked off a dispute that was to run for more than 300 years. The townspeople argued that Cirencester should be recognised as a borough. The key difference that this would have made was that with a borough there was a certain amount of self-governance permitted. Our learned friends argued over this for generation after generation. Jarndyce versus Jarndyce does not even start to compare. Many thought that the dissolution of the monasteries in 1539 would have returned power to the local townspeople but it was not to be. King Henry VIII decreed that Cirencester should be put under the governance of a Lord of the Manor.

It is not surprising considering all the resentment felt by the townspeople against the crown that when the Civil war came along that the citizens of Cirencester allied themselves to the parliamentarians while the aristocracy and clergy took the Royalist side. There was a battle fought between the two sides in February 1643 when over 300 were killed.

Cirencester boasts the world's oldest Polo Club. Cirencester Park Polo Club was founded in 1896. I must admit that I thought that the game was much older than that but when I looked into it the sport did not arrive in England until the second half of the 19th century. However I was correct in thinking that it was considerably older. Polo originated from Persia around the 5th century BC.

The town centre is full of old buildings. In similar manner to Stamford it has been able to keep the monotonous chain-store fronts at bay, giving the appearance of the old-style high streets that we used to enjoy.

While there are many fine frontages throughout the town, pride of place must go to the St. John the Baptist Parish Church. This elegant building dominates the market square. The perpendicular tower and the majestic triple storey porchway are the most striking features, but the whole edifice positively exudes excellence throughout its structure. The light-coloured stone shines its warmth across the Market Square.

The interior is no less spectacular, with its fan vaulted ceiling and numerous decorations. The church was built to reflect the wealth of the local wool industry of medieval England. St John the Baptist Church continues to achieve the ambitions of its founders to this day.

The path out of Cirencester passes by the Royal Agricultural College. This College was the first agricultural teaching establishment in the English speaking world. It was founded in 1842 and the Royal Charter was awarded in 1845. The college owns two farms. Coates Farm is mostly arable with additional facilities for the equine sports of polo and hunting. Harnhill Farm concentrates on cattle, pigs and sheep, but also grows forage crops and has a speciality towards encouraging organic farming.

My steps then follow through woodland before arriving at the parkland of Trewsbury House. This house is set within the earthworks of an iron age hill fort, although this is not immediately apparent to me. Almost immediately the path takes me through a metal gate and I am on the towpath of what remains of the Thames and Severn Canal. Just half a mile to my left is the official source of the River Thames at Thames Head (also known as Trewsbury Mead).

About half a mile along the disused canal I pass the ruins of Gothick canal round house and shortly after this the canal becomes full of water and serviceable. I have come to the end of the diversion and have arrived at the familiar welcoming sight of the Tunnel House Inn.

My diversion complete it is time to top up the fluid levels before returning home.

A rather long but satisfying circular walk can be made using the Cirencester diversion. Starting at Cirencester the adventurer can walk northwards up the banks of the River Churn passing through Baunton and North Cerney to Rendcomb, then follow the Macmillan Way through Woodmancote and Duntisbourne Rous to reach the edge of Cirencester Park. The circuit then continues through the park passing through Sapperton and Hailey Wood before emerging at Tunnel House Inn. From the Inn it is a mile along the tow path of the Thames and Severn Canal and then a further two miles to arrive back in Cirencester.

In all this circuit is nineteen miles long but covers two very pleasantly different terrains, ascending the Churn Valley and then passing through the well managed estate of Cirencester Park.

RENDCOMB TO AVENING

Rendcomb to Cirencester Park

As I start out from Rendcomb I notice that the weather seems to have blessed me again. There is a definite taste of spring in the air. Clear skies overhead are matched with a stillness in the air that seems to make everything this morning that little bit brighter. The forecast is very positive for the next week or so. Perhaps my daily struggles against the more hostile elements of our English weather systems will become a distant memory over the next few days. Here's hoping!

The uphill walk along the road to the peaceful small hamlet of Woodmancote certainly warms me up. There are some rather nice houses here with expansive well-kept gardens. This would be a very nice place to live and very convenient for commuting to nearby Cirencester. Attractive though this proposition may be there is no point in me phoning the local estate agents. Such high-end abodes are bound to be way above my budget level.

The Macmillan Way follows a series of paths, tracks and lanes before bringing me out at the embankment of the A417. This road follows the course of the old Roman road the Ermin Way which ran (or more accurately for the legionnaires marched) from Silchester near Reading to the Roman fortress at Gloucester.

At this point the guidebook goes into overdrive with staccato instructions to go left, right, under bridges, through gates, right, left, wood on left, through gate, wood on right, so many steps then turn again, twist, stick, ignore that gate but not the next one and so it went on. I was worn out just by reading it. My instinct was that I would be much better off simply using the map but that proved to be even worse. The standard 1:50,000 was no use at all for such short sharp changes in direction. Signs did you say? What signs? Some poor soul would have needed to bring a Transit full of signs to way-mark the route through this lot. There was nothing for it but to seriously concentrate on the book.

I take my sun hat off to whoever wrote this section of the MacMillan Way guide-book. The aforementioned lengthy passage which contained all of the directional changes ended with "over small bridge to left of ford crossing Dunt stream in attractive Duntisbourne Rouse hamlet". To my gratitude and astonishment that is exactly how I arrived at the tiny settlement.

The ivy covered gabled cottages by the ford make an attractive photograph. So too does the tiny church of St. Michael.

Wait a minute! Back-pedal a bit. Has the guide writer got something wrong after all? What is the difference between a village and a hamlet? I was always taught that one has a church and the other is a play by Shakespeare. (I can't resist silly gags). In truth it is a common fallacy that a hamlet does not have a church. The Concise Oxford English Dictionary only says that a hamlet is a small village, especially one without a church. It does not precisely say that a hamlet does not have to have a church. It also does not say that a village has to include a church either. Another myth exploded; and another gold star for the author of the guide-book.

The tiny church of St. Michael is perched on the side of a hill overlooking the Dunt stream. When viewed from the side at a certain angle the building appears as almost a wedge shape, with a stubby tower protruding at the "pointy end". St. Michael's Church can proudly trace its origin back to Saxon times. The chancel is Norman and the short tower was added in the 15th century. It is designated as a Grade I listed building by English Heritage.

The only thing left for me to do is to determine how the strange name of Duntisbourne Rouse came about. In the Domesday Book (which by now all readers should know was dated 1086) lists the hamlet as Duntesbourne which meant "stream of a man called Dunt". The suffix was derived a little later by the Le Rous family who were the Lords of the Manor. Simples!

Bathurst Estate

Just over a mile after departing from Duntesbourne Rouse I arrive at the gateway to Gloucester Lodge. This gate marks the northern entrance to one of England's greatest country estates, Cirencester Park. The park is also known as the Bathurst Estate, having been in the ownership of the Bathurst family for over 300 years.

The estate was originally purchased by Sir Benjamin Bathurst who was a very highly rated statesman and politician. Bathurst rose to the high office of Treasurer to James II and was also a Governor of the East India Company. He later became Cofferer to Queen Anne. Sir Benjamin purchased the estate for his eldest son, Allen Bathurst. He must have been a very generous father because he also purchased large estates for his other two sons, Peter and Benjamin. Peter received Clarendon Park in Wiltshire while Benjamin was handed Lydney Park in Gloucestershire.

In a similar vein to his father Allen Bathurst was also a skilled politician and was rapidly elevated to the high rank of Baronet by Queen Anne. Sir Allen was an enthusiastic benefactor and promoter of literature and the arts, befriending many of the top writers of the time. Principal among these literary friends were Alexander Pope and Jonathan Swift, both of whom were regular visitors to Cirencester Park. There is a folly in the park known as "Pope's Seat" where it is said that Bathurst and Pope spent many hours planning the follies and broad riding avenues that feature throughout the parkland.

Sir Allen Bathurst was driven by an obsession to develop the estate into one of the finest privately owned parks in Britain. The estate already benefited from magnificent natural forests, but these were further enhanced by the addition of the "rides" and open spaces that provide such magnificent views across the landscape.

Today the estate covers approximately 15,000 acres and is immaculately maintained. I am simply scuffling along the footpaths but I cannot help but notice how clear the paths are and that the gates are of a very solid construction. Walkers and horse riders are welcome on the estate during the day and there are clear notices marking the routes that must be adhered to.

The Macmillan way sweeps across the estate meadows, the terrain rising and falling with the folds of the Cotswolds. Woodland is never far away, tantalisingly screening whatever may lay behind the trees from my view. All in all I will be within the boundaries of Cirencester Park for almost six miles today until I emerge at the Tunnel House Inn.

I pass close to the lovely 17th century mansion known as Pinbury Park. At the time of writing it is available to rent. It has all mod-cons, hot and cold running water, superb location and mine for only £8,000 per month. I wish!

Sapperton Tunnel

The estate village of Sapperton was listed in 1086 as Sapleton. This attractive village is now a part of the Cirencester Park Estate.

The church is dedicated to St Kenelm who, although in these days is one of Britain's lesser known saints, was highly revered throughout the Middle Ages. St Kenelm had a particularly enthusiastic following in Gloucestershire, especially in the town of Winchcombe.

Just after leaving Sapperton I cross the Broad Ride. This is a wide grassy avenue that extends for 5 miles in a straight line from Sapperton to Cirencester.

Attractive though the village undoubtedly is, it is not what we can see around Sapperton that is of most interest, it is what lies underneath it. The 2.1 mile long Sapperton Canal Tunnel was a vital part of the Thames and Severn Canal. It represents a feat of civil engineering that was a major leap forward in its time.

The Thames and Severn Canal was first authorised by Parliament in 1783. Almost immediately there was a controversy regarding the tunnel that would be required to be constructed at Sapperton.

The problems principally centred on the requirements for the width of the tunnel. River boats used on the Severn were known as "trows" and measured 15 feet (4.6m) at their widest point. Thames barges were commonly 12 feet across the beam. Both sizes were much larger than could be accommodated by even the widest canal tunnel that had ever been built up to that date. This was the 7 feet (2.1m) wide Harecastle Tunnel built by James Brindley on the Trent and Mersey Canal at Kidgrove, Staffordshire.

The original suggestion was that the Sapperton Tunnel could also be just seven feet wide and that the trows and barges would unload onto narrow boats that then transport the cargo through the tunnel and reload on the other side. After much heated debate it was decided that they would "go for broke" by digging the tunnel 15 feet high and 15 feet wide so that it could be used by both trows and barges without incurring the additional handling costs of transferring loads at either end.

Excavation began in 1784 and it was a remarkable feat of engineering for that time. Even King George III came to see the work being carried out on the tunnel. The construction was not simply carried out "end to end" by starting at each end and meeting in the middle as you may have first expected. Instead 25 access shafts were sunk along the route enabling multiple work faces to be attacked simultaneously. The deepest of the access shafts was 244 feet (74metres) below the surface. It was a huge operation and thousands of "navvies" were required to carry out the work.

The tunnel was opened on 20th April 1789. It measured 3,817 yards in length (3490 metres) and was at that date the longest tunnel in Britain. Sapperton held this distinction until 1811 when it was finally overtaken by the 5,456 yards (4,989m) Standedge Tunnel on the Huddersfield Canal. Believe it or not after all this time, Sapperton is still the fourth longest canal tunnel in the UK.

There was no facility for a towpath through the tunnel so the barges had to be propelled by a method known as "legging". The process of "legging" was commonly adopted in many canal tunnels and was one of the hardest ways that has ever devised to move a boat. Two men would lie on a plank fixed across the bows with each placing their feet against opposite side walls of the tunnel. They would then walk sideways along the wall of the tunnel until they emerged at the other end. For short tunnels the bargees would usually do it themselves, but for longer tunnels teams of professional leggers were available for hire. There are many stories that some of the methods used to ensure that these teams were hired were somewhat aggressive. The end result was that leggers were required to become licensed in order to be able to ply their trade.

The Thames and Severn Canal linked the Stroudwater Canal at Stroud in the west to the River Thames at Inglesham. This link provided a continuous chain from the Severn to the Thames, and therefore enabled an overland route for heavy goods from Bristol to London and all points in between. The canal was fraught with problems throughout its life and required constant maintenance. One of the major problems was that natural springs would damage the clay lining and whole sections would be liable to drain away during a dry spell.

The final demise of the Thames and Severn Canal was the onward march of more economic means of transportation. The railways took away the majority of the business and when freight also began to use the roads then the death knell really began to sound. This section of the Thames and Severn Canal was finally abandoned in 1927. Roof falls have caused blockages in the middle section and also at the northern Daneway entrance meaning that the tunnel is no longer navigable through the whole length. Cotswold Canal Trust is currently proposing a restoration plan to re-open the tunnel.

The Macmillan Way follows the approximate line of the Sapperton Tunnel to reach the Tunnel House Inn. The path takes me over the hill and through the tranquillity of Hailey Wood. It is a very good path and although there are no Macmillan Way markers permitted on the estate the route is very clearly defined.

Tunnel House Inn was originally built to service the requirements of the thousands of navvies who were working on the Sapperton Tunnel. They must have done a roaring trade then with all of those men hot and thirsty from the sweat, dust and dirt of their digging.

It is not doing too badly now either. There is a steady stream of people arriving for lunch. The menu looks very appealing and I make a note to come back for a Sunday lunch and another walk in Hailey Wood. However, I am a bit warm and sweaty myself and it would be a shame not to slake my thirst in the traditional way observed by the navvies some 250 years ago. These old customs must be preserved, although I will bet that in the 1780's they never had any bright umbrellas to sit under!

From Tunnel House Inn there is a connecting path to somewhere that holds special memories for me. Just a mile away is the source of the River Thames and the Thames Path. This was the start of my first long distance walk and book, the 184 miles of The Thames Path, which I completed in 2008. (Quick plug for the book "Thames Pathway" available on Amazon and also for the website www.thamespathway.com).

Avening

From Tunnel House Inn it is six miles across the Cotswold countryside to the village of Avening. A pleasant walk through Gloucestershire pastures but nothing of any great interest to attract my curiosity. About a mile before reaching Avening I pass through a tiny hamlet known as Nags Head. This instantly conjures up a vision of anticipating a tatty yellow Reliant Regal (not a Reliant Robin as is popularly believed) in the pub car park and walking inside to meet Trigger, Boycie and the rest of the gang. Lovely Jubbly! It was not to be. The pub that had given the tiny settlement its name has long closed. "Boeuf a la mode"* as Del Boy would say.

(*"Boeuf a la mode"; expression used by Del Boy in his mangling of the French language when he really means "You win some; you lose some").

Avening is situated three miles north of Tetbury. It is the largest village in the South Cotswold area with a population of approximately 1100. The village owes its prosperity to the woollen cloth trade and boasted several mills that produced cloth until the latter parts of the last century. I have arranged for my "Dearly Beloved" to pick me up at "The Cross Inn". The pub has been recently refurbished and provided a perfect place to dine and have a couple of ales in the process. My good lady has not turned up yet and me and "mine host" quickly establish that at whatever time she arrives the official story is "I have just got here and this is my first one". We are clearly going to get along fine. I must come here again.

It is one of my general rules to strike up conversations with the locals and let them know what I am doing and that I will be writing a book about my travels. Often some very interesting stories emerge from this strategy, which is how I came to learn that to the best of anyone's knowledge the only church in England to be personally commissioned by a Queen is situated here in Avening.

We go back to the time just before the Norman Conquest. At that time the land around Avening belonged to a young man known as Brittric, Lord of Gloucester. Young Brittric was selected by Edward the Confessor to act as his diplomatic envoy for his dealings with Baldwin, the Count of Flanders. Baldwin had a daughter by the name of Matilda who duly fell in love with Brittric. For his part Brittric was not interested and rejected her amorous advances. Brittric completed his ambassadorial duties and returned to England.

Matilda was not a happy bunny. On the rebound she took up with the Duke of Normandy. The Duke, of course, was William who also seemed to have a bit of a score to settle with the English. Following his triumph at Hastings William crowned Matilda as his Queen. (You can see it coming now, can't you?)

As they say "there is no vengeance like a woman scorned". Matilda sought her revenge and persuaded William to confiscate Brittric's lands at Avening and throw him into prison. Brittric was consequently captured and incarcerated in Worcester Gaol where he was soon to fall ill and die.

Matilda suddenly was full of remorse and tried to make recompense for her part in the demise of Brittric. She set about building a church at Avening on the site of a former Saxon church so that prayers could be said for Brittric's soul. Matilda commissioned the building and made frequent visits to Avening Court in order to personally supervise the work. The church was consecrated on Holy Cross Day, 14th September 1080. To celebrate the event Queen Matilda gave a thanksgiving boar's head feast to the builders. This tradition is still continued to this day when the village of Avening holds its annual "Pig's Face Day".

The female connections at Holy Cross church extend to the current day. At the time of the walk (2012) the Rector of Holy Cross is the Reverend Celia Carter, who in 1994 was one of the first women to be ordained by the Church of England.

AVENING TO SHERSTON

Gatcombe Park

The Macmillan Way rises uphill again as I move southwards from Avening. It is quite a steep slope but I quickly gain altitude to be rewarded with clear views across the Cotswolds on another bright sunny morning.

To the north I can see across the valley to Gatcombe Park, home of Princess Anne, Princess Royal. The estate is probably best known for hosting the Festival of British Eventing which takes place on the first weekend in August each year.

The first farmhouse that I come to this morning sits behind a protective high wall but I can still see an interesting feature. The farmhouse has a clock tower with the clock clearly visible across the fields.

Chavenage

Chavenage House is some 200 yards away from the route of the Macmillan Way and I have to walk a little way along the road to be able to view it through the entrance gates. The house is an Elizabethan manor house constructed of grey Cotswold stone. It is privately owned but can be booked for hosting special occasions. The house can also be visited by special arrangement with the owner, Mr. David Lowsley-Williams, who will often conduct the tour personally.

Chavenage is an attractive building so it came as no surprise to learn that it is a very popular location for filming, both for television and the cinema. The fine stonework with its tall period chimney stacks has often been seen in the popular series "Lark Rise to Candleford" in addition to being used in an impressive list of films.

The first recorded tenant of Chavenage estate was Princess Goda, sister of Edward the Confessor. Goda married Earl Godwin, the Earl of Wessex and at that time the owner of almost one third of England. Godwin had his headquarters at Beverston Castle which is situated only a short way further along this walk. We will take an extended look at the life of Earl Godwin when we arrive at Beverston.

There are some even older records in existence providing evidence that the Chavenage Estate was also the location for the Hundred Court that sat during the 9th century.

Following the Norman Conquest the estate became integrated with the monastery at Horsley and things were fairly settled here during that period.

We will pass through time to 1536 and the Dissolution of the Monasteries decreed by Henry VIII. Henry presented the Chavenage estate to Thomas Seymour, who was later to marry the King's widow, Katherine Parr. Unfortunately Thomas Seymour managed to entangle himself in a failed plot against King Edward VI and was tried and executed for treason in 1549, his lands being made forfeit to the Crown.

After a short series of exchanges the ownership of the Chavenage Manor was transferred to Edward Stephens of Eastington. Stephens set about developing the estate and commissioned the reconstruction of the manor house in the classic Elizabethan style. Much of the glass for the large windows was alleged to have been recycled from the many redundant local churches left deserted following the Dissolution. Edward's son Richard inherited the manor following his father's death and he was responsible for installing many of the more ornate internal decorations.

It is to Richard's own son, Nathaniel, that we turn to for the most interesting aspects of the history of Chavenage. They involve two tales, one of romantic inclinations and the other a tale of sadness and ghostly apparitions.

Nathaniel was born in 1589 and was Lord of the Manor during the Civil War. He raised a regiment of horse to fight against King Charles I and took personal charge as their Colonel. In 1644 a branch of the staunchly Royalist Berkeley family were residing at Beverston Castle and it was decided that the castle should be captured and placed under the under the control of the Parliamentarian forces.

The task was given to the celebrated Roundhead commander Colonel Edward Massey who the year before had distinguished himself at the Siege of Gloucester (see my book "Discovering the Cotswold Way"). Massey twice threw his forces at the castle but was thwarted on both occasions. The Colonel could not work this out. How could the defenders be so well organised on both raids, when he had done his utmost to maintain the element of surprise?

This is where the romantic inclinations came in. Massey discovered that one of the girls at Chavenage was romantically involved with the commander of the Beverston garrison. When this young lady knew that there was not to be an attack that night she would put a lighted candle in the window facing the castle. The candle was a signal to her lover that he could slip away from his duties to spend the night enjoying her charms without being missed. Massey decided that with a small modification he could use this deception to his advantage. One night he lit the candle himself, waited until the castle commander came to see his lady friend and then captured him. Massey was then able to force the leaderless troops to surrender. I'll bet that the castle commander had fun explaining that one!

The second part of the Civil War story moves on to Christmas 1648. Oliver Cromwell knew that he had little choice other than to execute Charles I if he was to put an end to further Royalist uprisings. Cromwell despatched his son-in-law, General Henry Ireton, (who was also related to Edward Stephens) to Chavenage to request Stephens' signature on the death warrant of Charles I. For his part Stephens was not so sure that regicide was a moral and civilised solution. It took much persuasion (and probably many threats) before Stephens finally put pen to paper. Even after signing his name Stephens was still wavering in his opinion.

A few days later Stephens daughter Abigail returned from spending the festivities elsewhere. Abigail was horrified when her father told her what he had done. She flew into the most almighty rage and laid a curse on her father for his foul deed and condemned him for bringing their family name into disrepute. Edward Stephens was said to have immediately retired to his bed feeling unwell. He was fated never to recover. In a matter of weeks Edward Stephens was dead.

It is said that the family had gathered at Chavenage for Edward Stephens's funeral when a horse-drawn hearse arrived at the manor house. The hearse was being driven by a headless man. When the carriage stopped at the door the corpse of Edward Stephens stood up out of his coffin and walked to the hearse. Before climbing in to the carriage the deceased paid a tribute to the headless driver. As the hearse drove off the headless driver transformed into the form of King Charles I. Allegedly this scene was repeated whenever the male head of the family died, until the male family line was no more.

No carriage is available today, headless driver or otherwise, so I will have to walk the mile or so to Beverston Castle.

Beverston Castle and the Godwin Dynasty

The area to the west of Tetbury is fairly level and I can easily maintain a good walking pace. Across to my right there are the remains of Beverston Castle, one of the former defensive strongholds of this part of England, but now only a small remainder of its former glory.

Beverston Castle was originally built by Maurice de Gaunt in 1229. The wily Maurice flaunted the planning regulations of the time and initially constructed the fortress without obtaining the necessary permission for the defences. In the end he managed to gain the forgiveness of Henry III and the fortified castle walls were allowed to stand. For the next 400 years Beverston Castle would control this relatively flat area between Tetbury and the higher ground of the Cotswold escarpment to the west.

The next expansion of the castle was made by the Berkeley family, in particular by Thomas Berkeley (1293-1361). He had gathered together such a huge fortune from a combination of warfare and farming that he was known as "Berkeley the Rich". To stand out among his contemporaries as exceedingly wealthy must have meant that he was well and truly "minted".

The Civil War effectively marked the end of military service for Beverston Castle. We have already learned earlier of the two attacks made by Roundhead forces on the castle that caused considerable damage. Parliament decided that even though their forces occupied the castle in the aftermath of the case of the former Royalist commander and his "social excursion" to Chavenage, it was too much of a risk that the castle could be retaken by the King's supporters. Therefore Parliament ruled that the castle walls should be dismantled to make it impossible to re-fortify.

In earlier times Beverston was an important Saxon centre and became adopted as the headquarters of the powerful Earl Godwin of Wessex. Godwin had meteorically risen through the Saxon hierarchy creating a powerful dynasty that would be the major force in England during the turbulent times of the mid 11th century.

Godwin was probably the son of Wulfnof Cild, a theign of Sussex. The stories of his early ascendancy are somewhat vague, but his rise to prominence appears to have begun with his support for Aethelstan, the eldest son of Aethelred the Unready. When Aethelstan died in 1014 he bequeathed Godwin an estate in appreciation of his friendship and allegiance.

When the Dane Cnut claimed the throne in 1016 Godwin gave him his full backing and from this point Godwin's star followed a rapid rise. By 1018 he had become the Earl of East Wessex and within a further two-year period had taken possession of the title of Earl of All Wessex.

Cnut died on 12th November 1035 and the ruling of England fell into complete chaos. Follow this next part carefully. There were three main claimants to the throne; Harold Harefoot the illegitimate son of Cnut, his legitimate half-brother Harthacnut, and Alfred

Aetheling the youngest son of Aethelred the Unready. There were many twists and turns, plots and counter plots in the ensuing years as they tousled for the throne. Godwin was somewhere involved with the capture and death of Alfred to the advantage of Harold Harefoot. When Harefoot died in 1040 Godwin became an enthusiastic supporter of the claims of Harthacnut. When Harthacnut slipped his mortal coil two years later Godwin transferred his allegiance to Edward, the last surviving son of Aethelred. This resulted in Edward being crowned as Edward the Confessor, restoring the former House of Wessex to the throne. There was later to be a big downside to all of this chicanery. As a legacy from the thirty years that Edward had previously spent in Normandy the influence of the French at the English royal court was massively enhanced.

In the midst of all the upheavals Godwin was able to further increase his influence by arranging the marriage of his eldest child, Edith, to become the Queen Consort of Edward in 1045.

The rising Norman influence was not popular across the country. Godwin found himself as the major spokesman against the rising tide of French advisers to Edward. After several differences with the King, Godwin and his sons were all exiled in September 1051. Undeterred they were back within a year reinforced with a strong army and the backing of many of the lower orders of English society. This show of force manipulated Edward into restoring Godwin's Earldom and the former exile was able to resume building a power base for the benefit of his sons.

On 15th April 1053 Godwin died suddenly at a banquet in Winchester. Some reports say that he choked on a piece of bread when asked to pledge loyalty to the King but this is more likely to be a scurrilous tale put around by his detractors. Most probably Godwin died of heart attack or a stroke.

The male heirs then set about reinforcing their own powerful standings. The eldest, Harold Godwinson inherited the title of Earl of Wessex. Sveyn Godwinson worked his way into becoming Earl of Mercia and Tostig was helped to the seat of Earl of Northumberland. Leofwine Godwinson secured the smaller title of Earl of Kent. Between them they possessed all of the power they required for the next step of securing the throne.

Things started to go wrong for the Godwins during 1065. Tostig attempted to double the taxes paid to him by the people of Northumbria and this resulted in his removal and replacement by Morcar of Northumbria (who also happened to be Harold's brother-in-law). Tostig was exiled and found sanctuary with Harald Hardrada, the King of Norway. For his part Hardrada also had his ambitions set on taking the crown of England.

Edward the Confessor fell into a coma at the very end of 1065 without specifying his intended successor. On January 5th 1066 Edward died, but not before regaining a short period of consciousness during which he allegedly declared Harold Godwinson to be the next rightful King of England.

When the succession was announced the rival claimants swiftly swung into action. Harald Hardrada and Tostig joined together forces to invade through the north of England, while at the same time William Duke of Normandy gathered his army to invade in the south. Both were intent on occupying the throne of England.

Hardrada and Tostig defeated Morcar on September 20th 1066 at Fulford to reclaim Northumberland. Harold marched north and confronted the Norsemen at Stamford Bridge, (which at that time was not a football ground in west London but a key river crossing just outside York). Harold caught the invading forces by surprise and put them to flight. Tostig was among the fatalities of the battle.

By the time Harold had seen off the Norwegian threat William of Normandy had already put to sea. Harold regrouped his forces and marched towards the south coast to repel the invaders. We all know what happened next.

October 14th 1066 was not a good day for the Godwin dynasty. Three of the brothers, Harold, Leofwine and Gyrth met their fate on the battlefield at Hastings. According to legend and the Bayeaux Tapestry Harold was shot through the eye with an arrow. There is no record of this incident being preceded by a warning shout from a French commanding officer to a junior soldier, "Vous be careful avec le crossbow Pierre. Vous could have someone's eye out comme ca"!

So that was the end for the Godwin family. For fifty years they had schemed, plotted and fought their way to the very top of the tree only to see it all crash to dust in the autumn of 1066. For them 1066 was not a Good Thing*.

(*Reference to "1066 and all That" by W.C.Sellar and R.J.Yeatman. This was a spoof history of England first published in Punch Magazine and later in book form in 1930. Anything that gave benefits to England and the English people was classified as a Good Thing).

Diversion to Tetbury

The Macmillan Way passes to the west of Tetbury but there is a diversion which enables the walker to visit this Cotswold town for either a short visit or an overnight stop. The town route turns left off the Macmillan Way approximately half a mile after Chavenage and before reaching the A4135 which links Beverston to Tetbury.

Tetbury originated from an ancient hill fort that was developed into a monastery by Ine of Wessex in 681. In later days the fortune of the town depended on the wool industry and also became known for its brewery.

In common with several other towns in the Cotswolds that were founded on the wool industry the town became very prosperous. Also like its peers that wealth was poured back into the locality leaving us a legacy of fine town buildings.

Tetbury boasts two particularly outstanding examples in its town centre. Firstly there is the Market House which was built in 1655. The ground floor is a typical pillared open space, where traders sold their wares. The upper storey was used for meeting rooms. The second major architectural attraction is the Parish Church of St Mary the Virgin and Mary Magdalene. This church was constructed in the 18th century in a Gothic Revival style.

Most of the buildings in the town centre are 16th or 17th century. There is an abundance of bright hanging baskets, window boxes and potted floral displays throughout the town. It comes as no surprise to learn that Tetbury regularly features prominently in the annual "Britain in Bloom" awards. The town won outright in 2010 and is a regular winner of the heart of England division.

The town has many antique and bric-a-brac shops. However there is also a wide selection of specialist shops selling high class foods and "Cotswold Lifestyle" clothing and designer household products. As you may have expected with so many valuable properties in the surrounding region there seems to be a preponderance of "top-end" estate agents.

The old brewery is now occupied by a rather unique shop. "Highgrove" principally sells products from the Prince of Wales' Duchy of Cornwall estates. This appears to be a great attraction for tourists to Tetbury.

Tetbury Woolsack Races

It never ceases to amaze me when I come across yet another way in which a community has come up with a wacky sporting event to measure the physical attributes of their more energetic members. At Tetbury I find another example to add to my bulging collection.

Thirty years ago while wondering what they could do to occupy themselves on a wet Whitsun Bank Holiday afternoon a group of local geniuses came up with the bright idea of running up a steep hill between two pubs while carrying a 60lbs sack of wool. Woolsack racing was born!

There are some stories that this tradition started in the 17th century as a way for the local drovers to impress the womenfolk of Tetbury, but it was not until the 1980's that it became an annual festival.

Gumstool Hill has a 1 in 4 slope (25% incline) on the 290 yards between the Royal Oak and The Crown public houses. This was chosen as the original course for the race although the present distance is set at 240 yards. The heavy woolsacks are a regulation 60 lbs for men and 35lbs for women.

There are races for men and women, both individual and teams. The results are published as official records and the current records are;

Men   Peter Roberts (2007) 45.94 seconds

Women   Zoe Dixon (2009) 1minute 5.03 seconds

The event is held on Spring Bank Holiday Monday and is accompanied by a street fair.

The diversion to Tetbury is about five miles in total, adding around three miles to the total journey for the day. On the return to the path the route passes the edge of Highgrove House, home of HRH Prince Charles. I don't expect that he will invite me in for afternoon tea and cakes. I rejoin the MacMillan Way proper just before it enters one of the main features of the walk and certainly the highlight of the day.

Westonbirt Arboretum

I have been looking forward to the next section of the MacMillan Way. The route passes through the Westonbirt Arboretum, the star jewel attraction of the Forestry Commission.

There has been a history of managed forestry at Westonbirt since the 13th century when sections of woodland were used for coppicing. The arboretum was founded in 1829 by Robert Stayner Holford (1808-1892) who owned the nearby Westonbirt House. Holford was a wealthy landowner and also the Member of Parliament for East Gloucestershire. His vast wealth enabled him to indulge in his passion for collecting works of art and also take part in the then fashionable craze for discovering and collecting plants.

Robert Holford collected trees with great enthusiasm, landscaping the estate at Westonbirt as he progressed. The work was continued by his son, George Holford, who greatly expanded the collection. When George died in 1926 the estate passed to his nephew Earl Morley who continued with the development. In 1956 Westonbirt was handed over to the Forestry Commission and they have managed it ever since.

The arboretum covers 600 acres (2.4 km^2) and contains over 16,000 trees and shrubs. Westonbirt adjoins the Highgrove Estate, owned by HRH Prince Charles. It must be very convenient for him to have so many plants as next door neighbours. Very handy for having a friendly chat with them over the garden fence!

The arboretum has over 17 miles (27km) of footpaths running through it making it very accessible to the 350,000 visitors who take advantage of this wonderful piece of woodland.

As you may expect the Forestry Commission have a very "green" agenda. Part of this is that they offer a 50% reduction in admission price for anyone who cycles or walks to the arboretum. I have certainly walked here. I have walked 183 miles to be exact. I wonder if I qualify for a high mileage discount. It must be my lucky day because the Macmillan Way takes me into the enclosed woodlands by the back gate, so I don't have to pay a thing. There is a cautionary note in the guide book that states that if you intend to stray from the official footpath you should go to the ticket office and cheerfully pay up. Quite right too.

This is the first time that I have visited Westonbirt in the spring. I have visited the arboretum several times before but it has always been during the autumn. At that time of year Westonbirt is a truly marvellous place with the full glorious yellows and reds of the turning leaves. The Japanese Maples are particularly striking and are an essential feature of any visit to Westonbirt in October or early November.

In spring it is very different. There is cleanness to the views. Fresh, bright green leaves are filling the trees while vast swathes of the ground are covered with the soft blue haze of flowering bluebells.

Rhododendrons, Azaleas and Magnolias are starting to bloom. Birds are swooping in the air and chirping in the trees while butterflies and moths are flitting about their daily business. There have been 136 different species of moth identified at Westonbirt including the rare Mocha Moth that resides in Silk Wood.

There are over 2,500 species of trees and shrubs at Westonbirt. They have been brought here from all around the world. Most of the trees originated from temperate climates, notably in China, North America, Japan and Chile. Nowadays there is a full replacement programme carried out by the Forestry Commission where trees are propagated in the growing houses by using early cuttings and grafting.

Some of the world's most endangered trees have a home at Westonbirt. Of these species 7 of them are classified (in descending order of risk) as "critical", 19 as "endangered" and 54 as "vulnerable".

Every single tree is labelled with the species and an individual tree registration number. The labels are black, but the ones to look out for are the rare blue labels. These mark the 79 "champion trees", those specimens that are either the tallest or have the largest girth in Britain. Piece of trivia for the day; tree girth is measured at a height of 1.3 metres (4 ft) above the ground.

Trees, shrubs and wild flowers are not the only things to grow at Westonbirt. An unbelievable 1218 different species of fungi have also been identified within the grounds.

The Macmillan Way follows the Broad Drive through Silk Wood. This is a surfaced roadway running from north to south through the centre of the working woodland.

There are only a few people walking around today although I expect there will be many more at the weekend if this fine weather holds. It is an ideal opportunity to take full advantage of the many benches conveniently placed along all of the paths so I take some considerable time to traverse the route through the arboretum. I discovered a particularly pleasant spot overlooking the length of Broad Drive and I sat for some time drinking in the peaceful atmosphere.

Sherston

The village of Sherston is one of those undiscovered little gems. As it is situated off the major thoroughfares few people will have any reason to go there. This is a great pity because it has a wonderful wide main street that is lined with attractive limestone-walled houses.

Sherston dates back to Roman times. The remains of a Roman Villa built around 350AD have been discovered in a nearby field.

The first record of any notable activity at Sherston was in 896 when Ethelred, Ealderman of Mercia, passed through the area. The village was then known as Scorranstone.

A more interesting event occurred in 1016 when King Cnut was rampaging through the Saxon dominated area. At Sherston he collided with the Saxon army led by Edmund Ironside and the ensuing battle raged for two days. The Saxons were the stronger army and Cnut retreated back to London. At that time the leader of the local militia was John Rattlebone, who gave his assistance to Edmund Ironside. The name "Rattlebone" was said to derive from the effect he had on his opponents when he struck them with his great broadsword.

At the battle with Cnut's army John Rattlebone was fatally wounded. According to the local legend he carried on fighting by clutching a stone tile to his body in a futile attempt to reduce the flow of blood. Outside the porch of the Holy Cross church there is a weather beaten statue. Depending on how you want to view it the figure is either meant to represent a churchgoer clutching a bible or it is John Rattlebone clasping the stone tile so that he can continue to do battle. Rattlebone wins every time for me.

John Rattlebone lives on in Sherston by giving his name to The Rattlebone Inn. This was my sort of village pub. Built in the 17th century it has a labyrinth of nooks and crannies. Even at 6.30 it was filling up with all sorts of people in the bar and restaurant. The clientele covered all classes from the farm workers in their overalls through to the retired country couple out for their Friday treat.

There seems to be a lot of activity here judging by the pictures and notices on the walls. The pub has a skittle alley and three boules pistes. The Rattlebone Inn is also the headquarters of the "Ancient Order of Sherston Mangold Hurlers". This is allegedly a local pastime somewhat similar in nature to bowls only played with Mangold-Wurzels. More predictably it also seems to involve copious quantities of cider. Take at look at their website if you think I am making all this up as I go along.

I sat at a small table in the bar and ordered rump steak and settled down to sample the local brew. Within a very short time half a cow and a mountain of chips surrounded by vegetables appeared before me. It took ages to get through but I did it. Marvellous!

The question I most wanted to ask was who put their soundtrack together? It was every sequence that you could ever wish for. Who, Stones, Springstein and Cream all followed in quick succession, and then topped by Creedence! I just knew that if I stayed for another pint or two that the Kinks and Lynard Skynard would be playing at some point. Bang on cue "Sweet Home Alabama" was reverberating through the air as the barmaid handed over my third pint. As the man famously said, "I'll be back".

I have stayed in some different B&B's in my time, but I have not experienced anywhere quite like "Carriers Farm". Anybody who decides to walk the MacMillan Way simply has to stop here. It is only about a quarter of a mile south of Sherston and just a couple of hundred yards away from the footpath.

On the surface Carriers Farm describes itself as a farmhouse B&B set in 10 acres of organic pasture. That does not really do it justice. The three guest double bedrooms are in a converted milking parlour annexed from the farmhouse. The rooms are fitted to an exceptionally high standard with immaculate en-suite facilities. Nothing has been spared to provide the ultimate accommodation. It has everything; top quality soft furnishings, luxury towels, Wi-Fi, internet TV and quality branded toiletries.

The best is yet to come in the form of the breakfast. Everything was locally produced. There were local cereals, genuine home-made bread and a plate absolutely brimming with ham, salami and cheese. All washed down with a locally produced orange juice. The views from the breakfast room on another bright sunny morning provide an ideal appetiser for the day ahead.

SHERSTON TO BOX

DAY 13
15 MILES

Sherston to Castle Combe

My route this morning starts on the southern edge of Sherston at the stone bridge over the River Avon. At this point the river is little more than a stream, but when I next encounter this water in two days time at Bradford-on-Avon it will be a very different proposition.

The Avon and I are going to take very different routes on our separate ways to Bradford-on-Avon. I will be travelling steadily southwards, whereas the river will be making a giant loop out to the east before turning south and then finally twisting to the west. Incredibly the river only travels 19 miles as the crow flies between its source at Acton Turville near to Chipping Sodbury and entering the Bristol Channel at Avonmouth. By following the sweeping circle that it actually takes the river flows all of 75 miles to reach its final destination.

Indeed I initially find myself walking in completely the opposite direction to the flow, travelling upstream from Sherston to the village of Luckington. Luckington is a very quiet and rural place. Just on the opposite side of the village is the large and well-known Badminton Estate, the home of the famous horse trials.

The MacMillan Way now crosses a small region of poor quality ground. There is little of interest in the sparse fields. Unlike the grassy meadows and rich woodland experienced over the last few days the vegetation is scrubby, and some of the ground is quite boggy. The guide book advises me to follow the instructions carefully although I find little difficulty with the terrain. When the book directs me to "aim for a lone oak tree" and there is only one arboreal specimen in sight then that is obviously the right way to go. The track under the railway embankment is also easy to spot from a fair distance away so I simply stride towards it and ignore the other advice. Once I emerged from the short tunnel I could see my next landmark, the tower of Littleton

Drew church, in the distance. The path is very clearly worn into the ground and I soon arrive in the small village.

Littleton Drew is quite small. The name originates from the Saxon, Little Tun, which means "small farm". The suffix Drew derives from Walter Driwe who was the Lord of the Manor in 1220. A bench placed on the small green opposite the church provides me with a convenient seat for a rest before moving on. I have travelled five miles since Sherston and it has been very easy walking. Nonetheless, I am now 191 miles from the start, nearly two-thirds of the way with only 99 miles remaining, so the legs need looking after. Besides it is a very peaceful place to pause for a while. This is a lot more than I can say for the next landmark.

The quiet lane leading me out of peaceful Littleton Drew crosses under the busy M4 motorway. Fortunately for the villagers it is far enough away to save their ears from suffering too much from the constant drone of the traffic.

The M4 connects Chiswick, London with Pontarddulais which is near to Llanelli, South Wales. It is one of very few road transport links in this country that travel east-west and as a consequence becomes very congested at times.

Construction was first proposed by the Ministry of Transport in 1930 but they did not get around to issuing a plan until 1956. The first section to be opened was the Maidenhead bypass in 1961.

The motorway now runs for a continuous 191.8 miles which is an amazing coincidence. That distance is within a few yards of the exact mileage that I have covered so far along the MacMillan Way. Spooky.

I cross a small bridge over the little By Brook. I will be meeting up again with this stream a little later on. I will then be following it for almost eight miles to my evening destination at Box. Over to my left stands Lugbury Long Barrow, an ancient Neolithic monument. The arrangement that I can see consists of a large oblong stone placed on its side edge, seemingly resting against two upright pillars of stone at each end. The stones originally formed part of a original burial chamber. The formation is believed to be around 4,000 years old.

The path takes me over the Fosse Way then along a tree-shaded path before emerging onto a golf course. It is a Saturday morning so the course is quite busy with the weekend hackers. I keep a keen ear for the shout of "fore" to enable me to avoid being struck by stray golf balls. The course is very attractive with an undulating layout, and this is further enhanced by the twists of the By Brook across the fairways.

The golf course occupies much of the area once covered by the ancient Stone Age hill fort. The geography was ideal for a defensive location. Three sides of the hill are steeply sloping with only a narrow connection on the more level side. The fortification stood overlooking the valley thus giving the next village its name. Castle Combe means the "Castle of the Valley". The name Combe translates as the Saxon word for a valley. The Romans later used the same location for their own fort to help protect the Fosse Way.

After the Romans returned home during the 5th century the Saxons moved in. At least they did until the Normans arrived to evict them. The castle was enlarged in a "motte and bailey" design by Reginald de Dunstanville in 1140.

The path continues down some stone steps and I am treated to a wonderful view of what many people consider to be the prettiest village in England. A gap between two stone cottages provides a picture frame for the Market Cross and the surrounding limestone buildings of Castle Combe.

Castle Combe

Castle Combe is at the southernmost edge of the Cotswolds Hills, just 12 miles from Bath. The entire village is designated as a conservation area, with the limestone houses and shops all listed as protected buildings.

Whilst the village initially would have developed from people seeking the protection of the castle, the wealth of Castle Combe was generated during the Middle Ages by the wool trade. Local spinners and weavers would work in the village using wool gathered from the sheep that grazed on the Cotswold Hills. The swiftly flowing By Brook provided the power to drive the mills.

The buildings at Castle Combe are constructed with thick walls of Cotswold limestone and roofed with natural stone tiles. They are all kept in an immaculate condition by their owners who decorate them with colourful hanging baskets and window boxes.

I discovered that the houses had not always been kept in such a pristine condition. Shortly after the last war the local council were having a terrible struggle with the estate owner, Mrs Maurice. The houses were descending into a state of disrepair and the costs of making them good were proving well beyond her means. There was no alternative but to sell the properties.

In 1947 the entire village was put up for sale by auction in 42 lots. The Manor House (now a hotel) had a reserve of £10,000 but some properties were available for as little as £150. After 3 hours of the auction sale only three properties, including Manor House, remained unsold.

The White Hart sold for £7,500, The Castle Inn for £4,250, but most properties went under the hammer for only two or three hundred pounds each. The final total for the sale was £39,000. This does not sound a lot in today's terms, but was still a lot of money back then. Remember that the buyers also faced a considerable additional cost to bring their new residences up to the expected standards. The Manor House was later sold by private treaty.

The Market Cross with its water pump forms the centrepiece of the village. This old structure has been here as the focal point of the village since the 14th century. It is situated in the middle of the village with the Church of St Andrew directly opposite. The church was built in 1291.

A few yards from the Market Cross is a low stepped structure known as the "Buttercross". At first sight it may appear to be the stubby remains of a once proud building, but looks are deceptive. It is was in fact designed and built to aid the tethering and mounting of horses.

An unusual feature of the village centre is a small walled enclosure. This used to be the village pound where any stray animals were corralled and not released until their owners had paid a statutory fine.

Castle Combe is indeed a very attractive village. The title of "Prettiest Village in England" will always be a matter of some debate. During my various travels I have visited several places that lay a rival claim to that prestigious crown. Nonetheless Castle Combe must be considered among the front runners.

Following The By Brook to Box

This is going to be a day of two halves. The first half was over sparse and scrubby open ground, but the second half will follow the By Brook from Castle Combe to Box.

No sooner have I left Castle Combe than I enter a woodland conservation area. I have been warned in the guidebook that this section would be muddy, but it does not seem too bad despite all of the rains over the previous few weeks. The By Brook flows a little to my right but is still clearly visible through the trees. Overhanging trees make this section an enjoyable stroll through the shady woods.

I cross the stream at the pretty little hamlet of Long Dean. The hamlet is made up of a handful of stone buildings nestling in the peaceful wooded valley. After passing the last house the path rises steeply uphill using a sunken track. The pathway is very clear and I soon come to the small village of Ford.

The Brook has widened and deepened since I first came upon it, and the fields after Ford are obviously popular with fishermen. There are small wooden benches provided for their convenience. The reason for the extra depth becomes apparent when I reach a weir just above Slaughterford.

The church at Slaughterford was restored in 1883. It had previously been lying in a state of dereliction since it suffered at the hands of Cromwell's Army more than 200 years earlier.

There is a raised pathway through part of Slaughterford and a little way along this there is an old post-box. It is one of only seven remaining in the country that are marked as being commissioned during the reign of King Edward VII.

After Slaughterford the Macmillan Way returns to a sunken track through the woodland. The track is known as Weavern Lane and initially it has a hard metalled surface. This is obviously a ploy to lure the unwary wanderer further along the track because it steadily changes in character. The "lane" becomes unsurfaced, narrower, deeper cut and more disturbingly much, much muddier. There are entire areas of wet ooze that would have had me sinking in to mid-calf if I misplaced a single step. Progress was becoming painfully slow.

I was so concentrating on not losing my boots to the suction of the cloying mud that I completely forgot to keep my eyes open for the mystery shoes.

The muddy section of the Macmillan Way along Weavern Lane has been subjected to the pranks of a practical joker since the 1980's. One day a pair of stiletto heeled shoes appeared fixed to the roots of a tree. Nobody will admit to knowing who put them there. Whoever it was certainly put themselves to a lot of trouble in order to ensure that the footwear stayed in position. The shoes were bolted to a metal bar that in turn was screwed to the exposed root of a tree.

A few years later the shoes had almost totally disintegrated when they were replaced by a pair of bright pink knee-high boots. The brightly coloured boots were both filled with foam to ensure that they remained upright. When these too became ravaged by the elements they were replaced with a pair of white stilettos. Three years ago a pair of men's brogues were added to the display.

Locals claim that they do not know who is responsible for this unusual jape. I am disappointed to have missed seeing them. That is if they were still there. One thing is for certain I will not be flogging my way through here again just to see a pair of shoes.

The struggle along Weavern Lane leaves me without a sense of awareness as to how far I have come. It has taken so long to navigate my way through the ooze and slime. Eventually I pass the ruins of the former Weavern Farm and I calculate from the map that it has taken me nearly three quarters of an hour to cover the last three quarters of a mile.

I am pleased to say that from this point conditions underfoot improve dramatically. A combination of field paths and farm tracks takes me through meadows and spinneys alongside the By Brook. The waterway is by now more like a small river than a brook, with rushes and weed beds lining the bank sides.

Box

The village of Box occupies an area of seven square miles of the southern slopes of the By Brook Valley. The locality is celebrated for the quality of its natural stone and there has been quarrying here since the 8th century. During the latter periods of the 19th century the quarries around Box were some of the most productive in the world. Much of the stone used in the construction of the historic city of Bath just four miles to the west along the A4 originated from the Box quarries.

Box is also well known amongst railway enthusiasts. The Box Tunnel, built by the famous Isambard Kingdom Brunel, passes under Box Hill. The tunnel is 1.83 miles (2,937metres) in length and at the time of opening was the longest tunnel in the world. Thousands of navvies were employed for the construction of the tunnel. Work started in 1836 and was completed in 1841.

Brunel was an engineering genius. The innovation and precision of his engineering was such that he was able to lay claim to many "firsts" and "biggest" accolades. The first tunnel underneath the Thames (Thames Tunnel), the longest span bridge (Clifton Suspension

Bridge), the longest brick span bridge (Maidenhead Railway Bridge) and the first ship made of iron (SS Great Britain). Brunel's list of credits runs on and on. The design and construction of the Great Western Railway was probably his greatest achievement.

There are two notable points about the Box Tunnel which illustrate the unrivalled technical achievements of Isambard Kingdom Brunel. Firstly the tunnel was started from each end and when the two tunnels became joined it was discovered that the error in alignment was less than two inches, an incredible piece of precision. Remember that this was achieved by using old-style optical instruments, spirit levels and hand-held poles. There were no GPS and laser beams available to him in those days.

The second shows the sheer unrivalled brilliance of the man. Shortly after dawn on April 9th the Box Tunnel is illuminated with light from the sun. So what? I hear you say. Well, if I told you that April 9th 1806 was Brunel's birthday how would you consider it now? There are some people that say it is just a coincidence. All I will say is find yourself a length of parallel tube, look through it and see how difficult it is to line it up with anything. Now imagine that tube is nearly two miles long. How hard would it be now? What would be the odds against all of that being just a coincidence? Isambard Kingdom Brunel was pure genius.

I love the following comparison between Brunel and our modern technology. According to the Government the HS2 high speed rail link with take 18 years minimum to build. That is 18 years using high-tech borers, diggers, lasers, computers, the full works. Brunel built the Great Western Railway from scratch using picks and shovels while making calculations with just a pencil and paper. He completed the project in six years. I rest my case.

My resting place for tonight is "The Bear" in Box. It is very different to "Carriers Farm" having only the standard facilities. Nonetheless it is clean and adequate, and surprisingly low cost. The food was good as well. I ordered steak and kidney pie and it was of Desperate Dan proportions.

I then settled down in the bar to watch the Champions League Final between Chelsea and Bayern Munich. Bayern went 1-0 up, and then Petr Cech spectacularly saved a penalty to keep Chelsea in it. The biggest surprise was that Didier Drogba didn't fall over but managed to stay on his feet to score an equaliser with just two minutes remaining on the clock. Extra time and penalties resulted in Drogba scoring the last penalty for Chelsea to run out 4-3 winners. All in all an enjoyable evening in "The Bear" and a good warm up to the main football event of the weekend.

Two weeks previously I had faced a conundrum. Could I afford to take a day away from my walking schedule or could I manage to get to Wembley Stadium for the match of the season. For those blinkered by Premier League razzmatazz I am talking about proper football here. The Conference Play-Off Final between the mighty Luton Town FC and the hopelessly outclassed York City.

After suffering a totally ridiculous minus 30 point penalty and inevitable relegation from the Football League the great Luton Town were on their way back to where we belong. I really should be joining 25,000 like minded souls to cheer the Hatters on to their rightful destiny.

On the other hand I had a tight schedule ahead of me. I have limited time off work in which to complete my mission. Many other people have also promised their assistance and taken days off work to help me on my way. However much I animatedly pointed and tapped at my watch I would not be able to gain any extra "Fergie Time" in order to complete my task.

The upshot of all this is that tomorrow I will be walking from Box to Beckington instead of attending the great celebration of Luton Town returning home to their rightful place in the Football League. Come On You Hatters!

BOX TO BECKINGTON

Box to Bradford on Avon

It is straight into the hard work this morning as the MacMillan Way rises quite steeply out of Box up to the small hamlets of Henley and Blue Vein. This early exertion is followed by a gentle and leisurely stroll across fields and along narrow country lanes for the next four miles as I make my way towards Bradford on Avon.

I pass by the Elizabethan manor house at South Wraxall. The name Wraxall is derived from the old English word "wrocc" which meant buzzard.

The manor house is allegedly the first building in England where tobacco was smoked. According to the story Sir Walter Raleigh brought along some samples of his American discovery when he was visiting his friend Sir Walter Long immediately after returning from the New World.

It was just after I had passed along a track through Cumberwell Golf Club that things began to go astray. Everything was going swimmingly until the track from the golf course ended and the footpath allegedly crossed a few large fields. The farmer had obviously heard that I was coming and had deliberately ploughed all his fields specifically to cause the most annoyance to me.

The general rule in the countryside is that you must always try to follow the path. That rule applies even if that requires walking through growing crops or in this case over a recently ploughed field.

The trusty map and compass successfully saw me across four large fields to emerge at the correct gate but I was completely whacked in the process. I found it absolutely exhausting treading through the recently ploughed furrows. My boots sank up to the ankles with every single step. Progress was extremely slow.

It took a good while and many naughty words before I reached the relief of the firm pavements of Bradford on Avon.

Bradford on Avon

Bradford takes its name from the "Broad Ford" crossing of the River Avon that was used by travellers in ancient times. It is a smaller and quieter version of its near neighbour, Bath. After several days of peaceful solitude the bustle of a town is a drastic change of environment for me. I am not able to stroll nonchalantly down the middle of the road here!

The stone Town Bridge that stands at the site of the old ford is of Norman origin. It was widened to its current capacity during the 17th century. Two of the ribbed and pointed arches are still made of the original 13th century stonework.

The bridge features a small "lock-up" which was known as the "Blind House". This small building was used for the purposes of temporarily incarcerating any drunkards and vagabonds that dared to disturb the peace of the good citizens of Bradford. When originally built the lock-up was intended for use as a chapel. A drastic change of plan!

Bradford developed as did many other towns in the Cotswolds as a wealthy centre for the textile industry. Initially the production of fine cloth was very much a cottage industry but as early technology developed so too did the requirement for larger and more efficient mills. Bradford was well suited to house the new mills because they could be powered by the waters of the River Avon. This resulted in the spinners and weavers moving en mass into the factories. The textile industry in Bradford on Avon was also fortuitously boosted during the mid 17th century by an influx of Flemish weavers who brought their refined skills to the area. The main instigators of this massed immigration were Paul Methuen and William Brewer. A plaque on a wall in Church Street commemorates these two entrepreneurs.

There is an alleged connection with the now much larger city of Bradford in Yorkshire. During the 18th century the growth of the textile industry in Yorkshire was beginning to threaten the traditional cloth business of the Cotswolds. The Yorkshire cloth was generally considered to be of an inferior quality, often being made from shorter yarns or recycled materials and sold at a lower price. The name given to this material was "shoddy", which is where we obtained that term for something that is below standard. However, the more affordable Yorkshire cloth was rapidly becoming popular with the average customer. The wealthy mill owners of Bradford on Avon would not lower themselves to make the inferior quality cloth and in due course the inevitable happened. The southern mills began to struggle to find customers and one by one began to cease production. At the same time the mills of Bradford, Yorkshire, continued to expand and prosper.

The empty mills of Bradford on Avon became an attractive proposition for change of use to the rapidly expanding rubber industry. Several of the mills around Bradford on Avon became rubber processing plants making a variety of products for the automotive industry and agricultural machinery. The headquarters of Avon Rubber PLC is still here today although now situated in a purpose-built complex at Melksham, only a few miles from Bradford on Avon.

On this sunny spring day the narrow streets of Bradford on Avon are ablaze with colour. There seems to be hanging baskets and window boxes on every wall. It really does look a cheerful town.

Tithe Barn

Just before I reach the Kennet and Avon Canal I am going to visit the Tithe Barn. This is one of the largest examples of a tithe barn in England and was once part of the former Bradford Grange. The barn was constructed in the early 14th century and is built of stone.

A grange was a centre for the administration of some of the more remote estates of the medieval monasteries. Bradford Grange was a part of Shaftesbury Abbey, the largest and richest Nunnery in England. Not only did the estates generate their own produce from the lands but they also took a share from their tenants as well in the

156

form of taxes or tithes. People would bring their tithes to the giant barn as payment for their taxes. The word tithe derives from the term for a tenth because typically one tenth of the harvest or newly bred livestock was the annual payment demanded by the Monastery.

The barn measures 168 feet (51 metres) in length and is 33 feet wide. It is divided into fourteen large bays. The stone tiled roof is supported on gigantic "A" shaped wooden arched trusses.

On the north side there are two large porches, with two smaller porches placed on the opposing south side. Between the porches are the threshing floors, cleverly positioned so that the dust and chaff from the threshing would be blown out through the open doors.

In common with the rest of the Monasteries of England Shaftesbury Abbey was dissolved in 1539. The tithe barn continued to be regularly used as a normal farm barn until 1974. The barn is currently maintained and managed by English Heritage.

I cut across from the Tithe Barn to join the towpath of the Kennet and Avon Canal which the MacMillan Way follows for the next two miles. I was looking forward to a nice tranquil walk along the towpath but it was not to be. The reason was that my timing was unfortunate. As I marched boldly westwards, the competitors in the Bradford on Avon triathlon were breathlessly running eastwards on the same towpath. I ended up spending most of my time playing "dodge the athlete". The finish of the race was in the park near the Tithe Barn so these participants are almost at the end of their struggle. Some of them looked as though they were reaching their limits of exhaustion. Huh! Easy life! Try crossing newly ploughed fields pal!

Kennet and Avon Canal

The complete Kennet and Avon Canal is really two stretches of river joined together by a short canal link. The first river section is along the River Avon between Bristol and Bath. The canal link runs from Bath to Newbury, with the final section being the River Kennet to its confluence with the River Thames at Reading. This waterway comprises 87 miles (140 Km) in total, with the canal link being 57 miles long. The canal was finally opened in 1810 a little over 250 years after it was first proposed.

It is not immediately obvious why there needed to be an inland waterway link between London and Bristol. At first view it would seem to the layman that the best way to move people and goods between the two cities in olden days would be to use the sea. Unfortunately that would be a classic case of assuming that 21st century conditions applied back in the 16th and 17th centuries. Sea conditions around the rock strewn Cornwall peninsula were risky enough for shipping, but the greatest danger by far was the threat from the French Navy and the numerous privateer ships that infested the English Channel in those days.

The idea of an inland waterway connection between London and Bristol was first proposed in 1558. The Avon and the Thames are as close as 3 miles from each other at one point and the land between the two waterways was considered relatively easy to dig. Henry Briggs put forward some proposals in 1626, but following his death in 1630 things went quiet again. One of the problems was the fear of landowners that improved water transport would reduce their capacity to charge high tolls on their turnpikes, and also that lower cost food from the West Country would lead to lower market prices for their own produce. It just goes to show that nothing much changes over the years!

It was not until a survey in 1793 by John Rennie that things started to progress with a route being finally agreed. The Act of Parliament was passed a year later and the construction work began virtually straight away.

When the canal opened in 1810 the landowners fears were proved to be justified. Carriage per ton from London to Bristol was available at £2 9s per ton by canal, whereby the same transport by road would cost nearly £7. The canal offered an immediate advantage and prospered from the very beginning.

Unfortunately for the canal company they had left it far too late to fully capitalise on their investment. In 1841 Brunel opened his Great Western Railway and offered much lower carriage rates combined with a very much faster transportation time. Within ten years the tonnage transported by the Kennet and Avon Canal was slashed by half. In 1852 the Great Western Railway Company purchased the Kennet and Avon Canal and started to squeeze the barge operators harder in order to force more traffic on to their railway. Tolls were selectively increased, restrictions were placed on night time movements and barges were required to pass through locks in pairs. As you can imagine this encouraged more merchants to switch their goods to the more convenient and economical rail transport. The pattern continued and in 1877 the canal reported an operating loss of £1,920. There would never be another year when the canal operation made a surplus.

In 1926 the company applied to close the canal. Permission was refused by the Ministry of Transport who ordered that the canal should be adequately maintained. Following the Second World War the 1947 Transport Act saw the ownership of the Kennet and Avon Canal transferred to the British Transport Commission. Maintenance became more of a problem and within only a few years some sections had to be closed due to inadequate lock systems. The last full length passage from end to end of the canal was made by the narrow boat "Queen" in 1951.

The Kennet and Avon Canal Trust was formed in 1962 with the purpose of campaigning for the restoration of the canal. The following year the newly formed British Waterways took over the management of the canal from the British Transport Commission. Shortly after the handover the new management began work to restore the section of the canal near Limpley Stoke. The restoration continued in planned stages until after much fund raising and volunteer labour the canal was re-opened in 1990. Since that date many more locks, bridges and towpaths have been further restored. In 2011 the Kennet and Avon Canal was designated as a "National Cruiseway", putting a commitment on British Waterways to continue to maintain the canal along its full length.

The MacMillan Way follows the towpath for approximately 1.5 miles of easy walking. Without taking the triathletes into consideration there are still quite a good number of people walking here today. I soon discover why when I reach the hamlet of Avoncliff. The "Cross

Guns Inn" makes an excellent short walk destination from Bradford on Avon with the result that the beer garden is very crowded. The inn is believed to date from 1612 or possibly even earlier. It became a regular stopping point for the bargees providing refreshment for both the canal travellers and their horses.

Avoncliff itself was originally a mill village, having both a grist mill and a fulling mill. The fulling mill later became a flock mill, making lower quality cheaper woollen cloth.

Today the hamlet is best known for the Avoncliff Aqueduct that carries the Kennet and Avon Canal over the River Avon. The aqueduct is made from a combination of brick and stone. It was designed by John Rennie and is 330 feet (100 metres) long. There are three arched spans, with a central span of 60 feet (18.3 metres) and two side spans of 34 feet (10.4 metres) each. The stone did not give the lateral strength that Rennie had envisaged with the result that it kept sagging in the middle and required regular repairs. When the aqueduct was restored in 1980 a lined concrete cradle was inserted to reinforce the structure.

My route takes me under the aqueduct and then rises steeply up a winding footpath through woodlands. Initially I am able to enjoy some good elevated views back to the aqueduct but then I become enveloped by the trees as I leave the Avon Valley behind.

Iford Manor

At the top of the rather sharp incline is the village of Westwood. I only touch the edge of the village whilst passing through a quiet residential housing estate. I decide to take the short diversion to view Westwood Manor, a property that has been owned by the National Trust since 1956. The stone manor house dates from the 15th century and over the following 300 years has been considerably expanded. Inside the house there is a fine collection of period furniture and a collection of 17th and 18th century tapestries. Westwood Manor lays claim to be the owner of the oldest Italian keyboard instrument in the country. The instrument is kept in full working order. There is also a wonderful yew topiary garden that sets the house off nicely.

Meaning no disrespect to Westwood Manor, but I want to move swiftly on to my next port of call. I drop down into the steep-sided valley of the River Frome and arrive at Iford Manor. Walking down Iford Hill I can see the stone footbridge crossing the river, with the stone statue of Britannia perched on the centre of the parapet. That view alone tells me that there will be something special ahead. I was not to be disappointed.

Iford Manor can trace its origins back to medieval times. The Italianate facade and gardens that are seen today are due to the development work carried out by the architect and landscape designer Harold Ainsworth Peto who purchased the small estate in 1899. Until his passing in 1930 he designed and developed the house and gardens in his own imaginative style. This style was very much influenced by his extensive travels to Spain, Greece and Italy. Iford Manor contains artefacts that Harold Peto collected during his journeys.

The gardens are built on the steep hillside of the Frome valley and feature steps, terraces, sculptures and pools, all overlooking the wonderful views across the valley. A variety of footpaths thread their way through the valley allowing access to most parts of the estate.

The current owners have continued to preserve Peto's creation and the gardens are open to the public from April to October. During the summer months the cloister area is used for the performance of music recitals and small operas.

More importantly for my immediate needs there is a tea room serving a choice of refreshing teas and mouth-watering cakes. These are essential for anyone walking the through route from Avoncliff to Farleigh Hungerford, so you can imagine how vital they were for anyone who had walked here from Boston.

Saying a farewell to the ladies in the tea room I continue on my journey. I cross over the bridge, enabling me to take a closer look at the statue of Britannia. She is standing on the parapet gazing upstream towards Westwood, keeping a careful watch on the people as they walk down the hill towards her.

The MacMillan Way continues to follow the right hand bank of the River Frome. I pass an attractive weir, which according to the guidebook means that I am now in Somerset. This leaves just two counties to cross before the finish.

Farleigh Hungerford Castle

The ruins of Farleigh Hungerford Castle sit on a small hill. There are the remains of two ruined towers from the original four, the eastern gatehouse and some crumbled walls still standing.

The castle dates from the 14th century when the Inner Court was built between 1377 and 1383 for Sir Thomas Hungerford who was the Steward to the rich and powerful John of Gaunt. The castle was extended between 1430 and 1443 by his son, Sir Walter Hungerford. Sir Walter was a knight to Henry V and had become rich through his gains through the Hundred Years War.

The castle remained in the Hungerford family for most of the following 200 years. The family lost possession for a while during the Wars of the Roses. The Hungerfords were on the Lancastrian side and the castle was forfeited to the crown under the Yorkist Edward IV. The castle then passed to his brother, Richard Duke of Gloucester who, when he became King Richard III, handed the castle over to the Duke of Norfolk.

The grandson of the previous Sir Walter Hungerford, who also carried his grandfather's name of Walter, had committed his services to Henry Tudor. As a reward for his loyal support at the Battle of Bosworth Field the ownership of Farleigh Castle was returned to the Hungerford family.

When the English Civil War started in 1642 the castle was owned by Sir Edward Hungerford who declared for the Parliamentarians and became one of the main leaders of the Roundhead Army. The castle was captured by the Cavaliers in 1643, but was retaken by the Roundheads in 1645.

The last Hungerford to own the castle was also named Sir Edward. He had a penchant for gambling and expensive living which resulted in the inevitable fiscal consequences. He was forced to sell the castle in 1687 to cover his debts.

Through the early parts of the 18th century Farleigh Castle gradually disintegrated into a poor state of repair. Some of the stone was taken away for what is euphemistically described as "salvage". This expression usually translates that the locals took whatever stone they needed for the construction of their own houses.

In 1915 the castle was sold to the Office of Works, and finally to its current owners, English Heritage

Tellisford

In common with most of the villages I have passed through lately Tellisford was yet another former cloth village. The last mill at Tellisford finally closed in 1911. The original fulling mill has now been restored and incorporated into a rather fine modern house.

Tellisford is celebrated as one of the few "Thankful Villages". Thankful Villages are the civil parishes where all of the young men who went away to serve in the First World War returned home safely. The term was first coined by the prolific writer Arthur Mee (1875 to 1943) in his book Enchanted Land (1936). Arthur Mee identified 31 such villages in England and Wales, which have since been extended to 52 following further researches. There are no "Thankful Villages" in Scotland or Northern Ireland. When researches were extended to include France only one village, Thierville in Normandy, was found to qualify.

Somerset seems to have been particularly fortunate because there are nine villages in the county where all of the young men returned home. They are (in alphabetical order); Aisholt, Chantry, Chelwood, Holywell Lake, Rodney Stoke, Shapwick, Stocklinch, Tellisford and Woolley. Of these, Stocklinch and Woolley are "doubly thankful" having lost none of their people to the Second World War either. There are only 14 doubles in all of England and Wales. Amazingly Thierville also emerged from the second conflict unscathed.

There is a World War Two pill box sited just downstream of the mill. It seems a strange place to have one of these small fortifications. My researches revealed that this is just one of a whole series of pill boxes that were built along a line roughly 50 miles inland running from Somerset to Canvey Island, and then turning northward through Essex to Lincolnshire. The whole defensive structure was known as the GHQ Line, standing for General Head Quarters. The principal objective of the GHQ Line was to delay any invading German forces for long enough to enable reinforcements to arrive. Looking at the size of the defensive structure and looking at the wide area that it would have to cover I would doubt that Adolf's Army would have been delayed for very long. Perhaps it was a good thing that the GHQ Line was never needed to prove their usefulness.

Rode

When the River Frome approaches the village of Rode it develops something of a "wiggle". The meanders were ideal for the development of mills and mill pools so it is no surprise to discover that this was another busy centre for the cloth industry during the 16th and 17th centuries.

Rode had a strong reputation for the outstanding quality of its local cloth that led a little snippet of information that I will share with you. In the 18th century a national competition was held to manufacture a dress for Queen Charlotte who was the Queen Consort of King George III. The competition was won by a consortium of clothiers from Rode. During their submission work for the project one of the mills invented a new deep blue dye that was to be used for the dress. Due to the association with the royal dress this particular dye was authorised to be trademarked as "royal blue" and the consortium received a royal certificate to permit them to market the dye under that name.

A further point of interest is that the original royal blue devised by the clothiers of Rode is not the same colour generally recognised by that name today. Over the years the hue has gradually become lighter and brighter, with the result that the colour that we recognise as royal blue is now quite different to that originally used for Queen Charlottes dress. This can be seen if we look at the colours as defined by the four colour system currently used for most computer printers. Traditional royal blue is defined as 100 : 66 : 0 : 60 (parts cyan, magenta, yellow, black), whereas the colour recognised today is 71 : 53 : 0 : 12.

Beckington

My master plan was to reach Beckington before 3pm and then find a suitable pub that was showing the footie on Sky. I found the pubs all right but disastrously none of them were showing the game. Why had I not thought to bring a radio with me?

Plan B was swiftly concocted. This entailed calling up my brother, (who was safely in his seat at Wembley), and asking him to text me every time the glorious Hatters hit the back of the net. This would obviously be a frequent occurrence. Only two minutes of the match had gone by and the phone beeped. One – nil! Football League here we come. Come On You Hatters! Twenty minutes later, beep-beep. Oh yes, it must be getting better and better. What's this? It cannot be! The screen says one - one. Cheer up man, this will only be a minor hiccough. I must believe.

Just after half time and another beep – beep. York City have somehow managed to score again making it 1 – 2. This catastrophic news was followed by a long, l-o-n-g drawn out period of silence. By the time my "dearly beloved" arrived with the car there were only a few minutes left to play. Now that I had access to Five Live on the car radio things did not sound encouraging at all. Come on Greenie, say that we've scored, or got a penalty, or something. Give me the hope of a corner or a throw-in at least. It was not to be. Oh well, it's only a game.

BECKINGTON TO ALFREDS TOWER

DAY 16

17 MILES

Beckington to Nunney

There is a major problem with following guidebooks that were printed some years previously. Nature does not stand still. Nature wishes to spread itself as widely as possible. In short, things grow.

It is a glorious bright and sunny morning. There is this big orange thing shining in the sky and the weather forecast promises that today will be the hottest of the year so far. I am really looking forward to the hours ahead. Things began to fall apart after I had only travelled a short way out of Beckington. The guide book instructed me to follow a track alongside a hedge and then turn right when it came to an end. The path will then descend the hill side to a clearly visible bridge.

What the book meant, of course, was to follow the hedge until reaching the point where it ended in the late 1990's when these directions were first written. Where the aforementioned hedge ended now was getting on for half a mile further along the track. As the hedge now more resembled a dense line of trees I was unable to determine anything that was on the other side of it. More specifically I could not see any bridges.

I descended to the river after turning at the end of the "hedge" as instructed. There was no sign of a bridge anywhere. There also did not appear to be any other way out of the field that I was in except for retracing my steps back up to the track.

There then followed a frustrating series of ups and downs at every likely looking gap as I tracked my way back trying to find the right path. At the fourth attempt I found an overgrown gap in the hedge with a barely visible way marker for the MacMillan Way hidden among the foliage. I came out at the top of a field but still could not see the "clearly visible" bridge. A more careful survey of the River

Frome in the valley below revealed the very slightest end tip of a wooden bridge protruding on to the far bank. The rest of the bridge was concealed by a plantation that had sprung up over the last dozen years.

At long last I was over the bridge and on my way again. The River Frome had significantly increased in size since I had last seen it at Tellisford. Just upstream of the bridge was the very picturesque Beckington Mill, now somebody's magnificent riverside residence. What lucky people they are to live in such a wonderful location. I now say goodbye to the River Frome. It has been a delight to follow the waterway down from Iford. The river will continue on its journey through its namesake town, whereas I will be skirting around the western side of Frome using the scenic route.

Until the fatal moment that the arrow penetrated his eye the village of Lullington belonged to Harold Godwinson. Lullington has hardly grown during the last millennium, having a population today of less than 200 people. The village is attractive with a pretty green as its centrepiece. Standing by the village green is an old water pump which in days gone by would have been a focal point for the people of the village.

Orchardleigh Golf Club is quite busy this morning so I take great care when crossing the well manicured fairways. "Heading the golf ball" is not a healthy past-time. On saying that it must be said that as far as the people who I usually play golf with are concerned the middle of the fairway is by far the safest place to be. The most likely place to be hit by a ball struck by any of them would be at the edge of the woods or standing in knee-high rough! After safely negotiating the required holes without any mishap, the next stage of the pathway travels through Orchardleigh Woods. This is another section where the guidebook advises me to take extra care with my navigation. I do not find any problem and proceed quite happily.

Another walker gradually approaches towards me. He has two small flags flying from his rucksack proclaiming "Help for Heroes". As we meet he asks me if I am doing the MacMillan Way (my bright green "Macmillan" T shirt probably gave him a big hint). It turned out that he was doing the Macmillan Way from the opposite direction, from south to north, in order to raise funds for the soldiers' charity.

We compare notes of our experiences so far. Mostly we concentrated on the efficiency of the way marking and the state of the footpaths. I relate my tales of wading through the rapeseed, the extremely boggy bridleways and the cloying ploughed fields. My new friend responds with his own nightmares of missing markers, a very overgrown and impenetrable footpath to the south of Sherborne and a cautionary warning that at one point there was an electrified fence across the path with no alternative but to wriggle underneath it. Looking on the bright side we had both started at either end of the Macmillan Way and had met on the pathway so at least between us we had successfully navigated the whole 290 miles. Not quite the same achievement as Brunel's tunnel, but we had met nonetheless. We wished each other the best of fortune and carried on in our own directions.

Thomas Horner

At Great Elm I cross the Mells Stream. The water here has been dammed to form a duck pond and the residents quack their way towards me. They obviously associate walking humans with bags of breadcrumbs and noisily quack their demands for donations of food.

A short way downstream lays the village of Mells. I am not going to divert there, but thought that I would take the opportunity to share another little story with you.

Mells Manor was built during the period of the Dissolution of the Monasteries and there is a little tale to this with which many will find familiar if you think back far enough.

In the late 1530's Richard Whiting was the Abbot of Glastonbury. Whiting was a protégé of Cardinal Wolsey and he was becoming very aware that Henry VIII was seeking to overthrow the power of the monasteries and reclaim many of their lands in the process. Seeking to preserve the lands of Glastonbury Abbey as far as he could, the Abbott hatched a plan to hide the title deeds to several of the manors belonging to Glastonbury in a place of safety. His cunning plan was to conceal the documents in a giant Christmas Pie which he would send to his associates in London. The safe passage of the pie was entrusted to his faithful steward, one Thomas Horner.

Do I hear the tinkle of bells?

Allegedly Thomas Horner was not so faithful and trusty. He allegedly opened up the pie before reaching his final destination and extracted the deeds to Mells Manor. These he tucked away for himself as a reward for his services. If you recall the rhyme he "put in his thumb, and pulled out a plum, and said what a good boy am I". So did he take the deeds because he thought he deserved them? Perhaps the documents for Mells Manor just conveniently fell into his hands? Maybe he simply took them (as some may generously say) to "cover his expenses"?

The Horner family subsequently strongly denied any wrongdoing, but never let facts get in the way of a good story. What is certain is that Thomas Horner somehow acquired the title to Mells Manor and built a fine house.

Richard Whiting was fated to be the last Abbot of Glastonbury. Whitely was captured by the Royal Commissioners who held him on some trumped-up charges of robbing his own church. He must have known things were not going to go well when he read his arrest papers which ordered him to be "imprisoned then executed" even before his trial had taken place. You will not be surprised to hear that he came to a grisly end. He was forcibly taken to Glastonbury Tor where he was hung, drawn and quartered on 15th November 1539. Abbott Richard Whiting was beatified by the Roman Catholic Church in 1895.

Nunney

Nunney is another exceptionally attractive village with a stream, the Nunney Brook, running through it.

Nunney is named after a former Saxon chief, Nunna, and simply means "Nunna's people". The Domesday Book simply calls the settlement "Nonin" and records the manor as being in the hands of William de Mayen who was installed as Lord of the Manor by William the Conqueror.

The main attraction of Nunney is the unusually designed Nunney Castle. If we were in France there would be nothing out of the ordinary with the architecture, but on this side of the channel it is a rare building.

Nunney Castle was commissioned by Sir John Delamere in 1373. Sir John had studied the design of French fortifications during his military exploits during the Hundred Years War. When he found the opportunity to design his own castle he copied many of the key French features.

One distinguishing feature was his use of machicolations. This was a defensive feature discovered by the Crusaders in the Holy Lands. The Crusaders in turn introduced them into the design of the castles of medieval Europe. With this defensive structure the battlement juts out as a balcony around the top of the wall. Gaps are created in the balcony floor between the horizontal supports. Defenders are then able to drop rocks, boiling oil and hot tar onto any enemy soldiers at the foot of the wall without risking exposure to hostile arrows. The word machicolation is derived from the Old French "mache col" meaning to crush necks.

The castle was eventually purchased by the Prater family around the year 1560. The last owner of the castle was Sir Richard Prater who held it during the early years of the Civil War until 1645.

During the Civil War the Parliamentarians put a high premium on capturing Nunney Castle because they believed (wrongly as it was later discovered) that there was a large stock of weapons and ammunition held in the armoury. Two regiments commanded by Lord Fairfax were despatched to capture the fortress. Nunney Castle was besieged for two days until continued canon fire breached a large hole in the north defensive wall. At this point Colonel Prater decided that his best option to preserve what remained of his property was to change sides and pledge his undying allegiance to Cromwell.

Colonel Prater's treachery was not rewarded. Parliament ordered that Nunney Castle be "slighted". This is one of those understated words that are used to hide the true extent of the associated action. Far from being slight, the action meant that the castle was wrecked to such an extent that it would be rendered totally unusable for further military purposes. In the case of Nunney the interior was stripped out, the roofs removed and the Colonel's possessions deemed forfeit to the Roundhead cause.

All that is left of the castle now is the remains of the main keep and its surrounding moat. The keep has four round towers with conical roofs. The projecting battlements are still clearly visible. Nunney Castle is currently managed by English Heritage and is open for visitors.

The attractive stream-filled valleys that I have been walking through during the last few miles have made for a very pleasant section of the trail. It is very difficult in such situations to forget that this terrain is almost entirely down to the activities of man and is not the natural order of things.

It is not commonly recognised that the great British landscape with which we are all familiar is almost all artificial. Two thousand years ago this region would have been a very different place. Everywhere would have been covered with thick forest. The delightful valleys would have been muddy swamps and instead of being the preferred walking route for people like me would have been completely avoided by our ancestors. They would have kept to the dry ridges or higher hillside routes. The valleys would have been very uncomfortable and even the Romans seemed to have given them a wide berth. There has been a Roman Villa discovered just to the north of Nunney, but otherwise they kept very close to their own roads.

All this changed when the Roman legions left Britain. The law and order that they had imposed and reinforced swiftly degenerated as the barbarians gradually took over. Britain was plunged into the dark ages. Safety from the marauding bands of looters and pillagers soon became a necessity for many of our ancestors. Secluded clearings in the forest provided an extra element of security for settlements. They were difficult to find and the surrounding lands made the movement of raiding parties much more difficult. More low lying forest areas were cleared and farmsteads and small villages began to appear across the country.

In time the insular living of the Dark Ages began to fade, and the various Kingdoms of England started to emerge. This part of the country began to be more settled under the influence of the Saxons and gradually more of the valleys were cleared for livestock and arable crops. Steadily the managed landscape evolved over hundreds of years into the beautiful green pastureland and woodlands that we have today.

The next village is Trudoxhill which I mention only because this is the last village that I will be passing through for fourteen miles. From here the Macmillan Way travels across open countryside before taking me through nearly six miles of woodland and then followed by more open country until I reach the small town of Bruton. During the planning of the walk this section caused me the most headaches. There did not appear to be a logical place to stop overnight. I finally decided that I would arrange to be picked up this evening at Stourhead and resume from Alfred's Tower in the morning.

Silage

Walking towards Witham Woods I am able to catch glimpses of the top of Alfred's Tower poking above the trees. It looks a long way off, but the walking from here is very easy and I will soon eat up the intervening miles. The terrain now is open farmland and the warm weather over the last few days has changed the conditions underfoot to firm. During the afternoon I also encounter the first harvesting of the year. The recent days have been dry enough to enable the first silage cuts to be made and the farmers are working hard to gather the crop before the weather can change again.

Silage is much misunderstood by many of the people who visit the countryside. Fields smothered with giant black wrapped cylindrical bales or a huge pile in a farmyard covered in polythene and held down by old tyres are not among the most attractive of rural sights. However these eyesores are practical solutions that are vital for the farmers' livelihood. Let us now take a look at the process of making silage.

For a start, what is silage and why is it preferred to hay? Well, silage is a fermented high quality feed for livestock. It is mostly used for ruminants such as cattle and sheep. It is far superior than hay for retaining its essential nutrients during storage, and silage is also more easily digested by the animals. If you want a simpler description just imagine silage as pickled grass.

The main grass crops used for silage are maize and sorghum, but any of the cereal plants could also be used. It is not important for the crop to develop its grain as the whole plant is used for the silage process.

The first cut in late May is the most important because the early season grass is much richer in food content. The early growth produces leaf rather than the seed of the later summer. Ideally the cut is made when the crop is about 2 feet (60cm tall).

The moisture content is all important if the silage is to be of the best quality. To enable the crop to dry the grasses are cut and left lying on the fields for two or three days. This will reduce the moisture level to between 50% and 60% before undergoing bulk fermentation in silos or farmyard clamps. For making smaller silage bales of around 4 feet (1.3m) in diameter a dryer grass of 30% to 40% moisture is required. The grass for this silage is left to dry on the fields for a few more days.

Now that we have our grasses containing the right moisture content it is time to gather them up. Usually this involves a type of mowing machine that will gather the grasses, chop them up into lengths of around ½ inch (1.3cm) and deposit them into a cart or a baler.

The cart takes the cuttings to the farmyard where they are either transferred to a silo tower or piled into a big heap known as a clamp. When complete the clamp is covered with black polythene film and weighted down. This is where the tyres come in. Farmers have learned by experience that old tyres are the best way of keeping the covering film securely held down in all weathers while also providing the flexibility to adjust the covering when necessary.

For the bales the cuttings are tightly wound in a baling machine and covered in at least four layers of 25 micron plastic film.

The fermentation process starts almost immediately. During the first part of the fermentation the free oxygen trapped in the cuttings is used up. This takes about three days. The second part of the process is anaerobic fermentation where the bacteria present start to work on breaking down the complex sugars of the crop. This stage is often assisted by the farmer inoculating each batch with selected micro-organisms to assist the work of the natural organisms. The anaerobic fermentation takes at least a further two weeks to complete.

The making of silage involves some hidden dangers that every year are responsible for injuries and even fatalities. The dangers of industrial cutting machines are usually apparent, but there are other serious hazards. The fine dust produced is explosive, and there are many instances of explosions occurring as silos are filled. Another great danger is that of workers falling into silos. Due to the fermentation process any air in a silo is virtually devoid of oxygen. Anyone falling into the silo or attempting a rescue incurs a very high risk of being asphyxiated very quickly. Silos can be very dangerous places.

The fields I am walking through here are big, and there is a succession of tractor-pulled carts taking away the silage to the collection yard. The contractors will no doubt be working many long hours to completely clear these fields while the weather is good.

Witham Priory and Saint Hugh

The lands I am crossing were once owned by Witham Priory, one of the great Carthusian Monasteries of medieval times. Nothing now remains of this great ecclesiastical institution, but in its heyday it was one of the greatest institutions in all of England.

174

The Carthusians were a very strict monastic order. They were founded in 1084 by St Bruno of Cologne. They took their name from the Chartreuse Mountains in France where Bruno founded his first monastery. The order operated in an isolated manner. They had a strong belief in their own secluded society, but within their own groups led an individual and almost hermit like existence. They spent all their time in solemn prayer, copying manuscripts and carrying out essential agricultural and domestic work. Unlike many other religious orders they did not spend much time "spreading the word", preferring instead to concentrate on their own devotions.

There were only ever nine Carthusian Monasteries in England. They were also popularly known as "Charterhouses", derived from their Chartreuse origins. The nine Charterhouses (of which Witham was the first) were situated at Witham, Hinton (Somerset), Kingston upon Hull and Mountgrace (Yorkshire), Coventry (Warwickshire), Sheen (Surrey), Beauvale (Nottinghamshire), Epworth (Lincolnshire), and Charterhouse (London).

The Carthusian monks did not even want to settle at Witham in the first place. To understand the development of the Priory we must go back to a time where very different standards of conduct existed for both noblemen and men of the church.

On 29th December 1170 the Archbishop of Canterbury, Thomas a Beckett, was murdered by four knights in Canterbury Cathedral. The knights believed that they were acting on the orders of King Henry II who had exclaimed "Who will rid me of this turbulent priest?" The knights promptly rode off to Canterbury and put an end to the Archbishop. Henry later claimed that his outburst was only meant to be an expression of annoyance at the church meddling with Henry's plans, not that he wanted Thomas a Beckett permanently disposed of.

In medieval times it was common for noblemen to seek absolution for their sins by joining the Crusades or other Holy battles against non-Christians, such as against the Moors. In 1172 Henry II accepted a punishment from the Pope to serve three years in the Holy Land as penance for instigating the murder of Thomas a Beckett. When this penance had still not even begun by the end of 1175 Henry accepted an alternative punishment of founding three new ecclesiastical centres. He greatly expanded Waltham Abbey by bringing in many Augustinian Monks, developed Ambresbury (Essex) as a Convent, and promised to found a new priory at Witham.

The Priory at Witham did not start off well. The monks who arrived during the early years found a poor structure that was under-funded and bestowed with inadequate resources. The first two priors to be appointed both became quickly disillusioned and soon departed for pastures new. Henry was coming under immense pressure from the Pope to deliver on his promises. He had heard very high recommendations of a young monk at the Grand Chartreuse near Grenoble, a certain Hugh of Avalon. Anxious to get the church off his back as quickly as possible Henry sent a strong delegation to Grand Chartreuse to recruit young Hugh for Whitham. Initially Hugh did not want to know, and rejected the King's approaches. Eventually through a combination of pressures from Henry, senior figures in the Carthusian Order and the Papal Authorities, Hugh finally agreed to become Prior of Witham in 1180.

Hugh must have been one of those people who was powered by Duracell. He just would not stop. Henry must have wondered what had hit him. Hugh continually pestered the King for whatever he needed to develop the Priory. More funding, more land, more monks, more of everything. On 6th January 1182 Henry conceded to the demands and granted a Royal Charter to Witham Abbey giving it everything Hugh had asked for.

Witham expanded rapidly under Hugh's direction. While officially it was King Henry II who founded the Priory it would have remained insignificant if it were not for Hugh of Avalon. Hugh continued to be a thorn in the royal side and when he was offered the position of Bishop of Lincoln in 1186 he just wondered if this was what the cardinals at Lincoln really wanted or was Henry simply trying to get him out of the way? He solved that conundrum by going to Lincoln and organising his own secret ballot among the clergy at Lincoln. When he was unanimously confirmed as their choice he finally accepted the position.

If the monarchy thought that this was the end of its confrontations with Bishop Hugh they quickly had to have a rethink. Hugh refused to have any of the King's "yes men" foisted upon him in various roles, preferring to make his own thoroughly researched appointments for the diocese. He constantly championed the sick, the poor and the oppressed. Neither was Hugh a "stay at home bishop", for he travelled widely.

Bishop Hugh also enlarged Lincoln Cathedral. Although the Gothic masterpiece was not completed until well after his death Hugh was the driving force behind it being the magnificent edifice it is today.

How did Hugh manage to stand firmly against Henry II? The story becomes even more impressive when it is realised that Hugh was also Bishop of Lincoln through the reign of Richard the Lionheart and also that of the utterly devious King John. None of these three holders of the English crown were known for their humility and tolerance. The answer is that Hugh was extremely skilled in the arts of tact and diplomacy and was able to convince his monarchs that everything would be to their benefit. He probably led them all to believe that it was the King's idea in the first place. This probably teaches us all that nothing ever changes!

The emblem of St Hugh is a white swan. The story behind the emblem is that St Hugh befriended a swan, and the swan reciprocated by guarding him, following Hugh around the cathedral, and even standing guard while Hugh slept.

Hugh's diplomatic skills were much admired by his sovereigns and he was often called upon to help them out in their times of difficulty. It was during a diplomatic mission to France on behalf of King John that Hugh caught hold of an illness that culminated in his death a few weeks later on November 16th 1200.

St Hugh was canonised by the Roman Catholic Church in 1220. His commemoration day is November 17th. In recognition of his reputation for protecting the sick and the poor St Hugh was acknowledged as the patron saint of the sick. He is also the patron saint of shoemakers, and also from his emblem he is the patron saint of swans.

St Hugh's College Oxford is named in his honour. A statue outside the college library shows St Hugh carrying a model of Lincoln Cathedral in his right hand, whilst his left hand rests on the head of a swan.

St Hugh built up two great institutions that have fared very differently since 1200. Lincoln Cathedral stands proudly as one of the greatest ecclesiastical buildings in Britain. Of the great Witham Priory there is nothing remaining here today to show that it ever existed.

Alfred's Tower

The next five miles are through woodlands. The paths are clear and well marked, but as you can imagine the views become somewhat limited, mostly consisting of trees. On a warm and sunny afternoon the cooler shade of the woods provides me with more than adequate compensation for the restricted lines of sight. After about an hour and a half I can see the clear passage through to the top of Kingsettle Hill. Standing proudly at the summit at the end of the clear avenue through the woods is the magnificent stone folly known as Alfred's Tower.

Cast your mind back to Day Two when we arrived at Guthrum Gowt on the wide open fens. There we learned that King Alfred finally defeated Guthrum and his Danish forces at the battle of Ethandun in May 878. Alfred's Tower marks the former site of "Egbert's Stone" where Alfred gathered his armies together before the battle of Ethandun. Ethandun is now known as Edington and is situated a little south east of Trowbridge, Wiltshire.

It took 900 years for the memorial to be erected. It was the brainchild of Henry Hoare II (1705 to 1785) who at the time was developing the impressive Stourhead Gardens (of which more later). Hoare did not even build the monument as a memorial to Alfred, but to celebrate the end of the "Seven Years War".

The Seven Years War is one of the lesser known wars, but had great significance for the definition of current national boundaries. It was arguably the first "World War" because the hostilities were spread out over Europe, North America, South America and even extended to parts of India and the Philippines. It is also one of those trick questions beloved by pub quizmasters. Using your best Jeremy Paxman impression voice say "Starting in 1754 in which year did the Seven Years War end?" As soon as you have heard 1761 you can shake your head, look down your nose and contemptuously say "No, 1763".

The mess over its name is indicative of the total shambles that this war represented. In simple form it was a dispute between Great Britain allied with the Hanoverians against the Bourbons of France coupled with Spain. The dispute was not just about ownership of land, but trade terms, trade routes, alliances and all sorts of political shenanigans. The Prussians and the Portuguese sided with us good guys, whilst the Russians, Swedes, Austrians and various representatives of the Holy Roman Empire also piled in with their four penny worth, some of them changing sides at various times during the conflict.

As life is too short we will skip over all of the various battles except to say that there were many of them and all were very fiercely contested and suffered high casualty rates.

There were several treaties that redistributed lands at the end of the war. Great Britain and Prussia were the major beneficiaries, mostly at the expense of France and the Holy Roman Empire. France lost control of Canada, several Caribbean Islands and any influence that they had in India. Spain lost Florida but gained parts of Louisiana.

To commemorate the end of all of this mayhem Henry Hoare commissioned Henry Flitcroft to build the tower. The work was completed in 1772. It reaches 160 feet high (49m). The floor shape is triangular in section with rounded tower projections at each of the angles. One of the towers contains a spiral staircase with 205 steps leading to the roof with its crenulated parapet. The red brick walls are 2 feet 9 inches (84cm) in thickness.

Above the Gothic entrance door there is a statue of King Alfred. Underneath it there is the following inscription. "Alfred the Great AD 879 on this summit erected his standard against Danish invaders. To him we owe the origin of juries, the establishment of a militia, the creation of a naval force. Alfred, the light of a benighted age, was a philosopher and a Christian, the father of his people, the founder of the English monarchy and liberty."

The tower is open to the public from mid-March to October on Saturdays, Sundays and Bank Holidays. On a clear day it is claimed that you can see for up to 50 miles from the rooftop platform.

Diversion to Stourhead (Additional 2 miles + Gardens.)

There is an alternative route for the day that I am going to take now. At first you may think this is strange thing to do but by the time I have finished you may have seen the logic of it. I am going to walk from Alfred's Tower to the beautiful Stourhead Gardens and finish my day there. I will resume the Macmillan Way again at Alfred's Tower tomorrow.

The route takes me through the woodlands, dropping down to go around the southern end of the Stourhead Lake before walking up the road into the village of Stourton.

Stourhead is one of the great English estate gardens, some would go so far as to say this is definitely the best.

The gardens were first opened in 1740 to great acclaim. The estate covers 2,650 acres (1,072 hectares). Most of the estate is ancient woodlands, chalk downs and farmland. However it is the lake and gardens that are the best known. The lake is surrounded by follies. Small temples in the classic design and intriguing grottos reveal themselves as I make my way around the lake. There is the iconic picture of Stourhead that everyone has probably seen at some time or other. It depicts the classic Parthenon standing among the trees, with the reflection shining in the waters of the lake.

Old Staunton House was purchased by wealthy banker Henry Hoare in 1717. He immediately demolished the house and replaced it with the Colen Campbell designed Palladian mansion of Stourhead House. Following the death of Henry Hoare in 1725 the development of the house was continued by his son, Henry Hoare II.

The development continued with Richard Colte Hoare who lived in the mansion between 1795 and 1820. He commissioned the celebrated cabinet maker Thomas Chippendale the Younger to fill the house with bespoke furniture, much of which is still able to be viewed by visitors to the stately home.

The follies for which the gardens are most noted were designed and built by Henry Flitcroft, who we have already heard was the designer of Alfred's Tower. He built the Temple of Ceres in 1744 and added the Temple of Hercules in 1754 and the Temple of Apollo in 1765. As previously mentioned the tallest of them all, Alfred's Tower, was completed by Henry Flitcroft in 1772.

The walk around the lake takes about an hour and a half allowing for time to sit and take in the views. Don't be tempted to rush round Stourhead. If you do you will miss out on one of the most attractive National Trust estates that I have ever visited.

The house was passed into the ownership of the National Trust in 1947.

That is it for the day. It has been a long day with the additional walk to Stourhead combined with the loop around the lake but it was well worth the extra exertions to finish the day at such a wonderful place.

ALFRED'S TOWER TO SOUTH CADBURY

DAY 17

17 MILES

John Leland and the Leland Trail

My walk today will be along part of a longer route known as the Leland Trail. This 28 mile pathway starts at Alfred's Tower and travels to Ham Hill Country Park. Ham Hill is located a little to the west of Yeovil and is the site of an ancient hill fort. I will be following the Leland trail for 17 miles until I reach South Cadbury.

The Leland Trail has been developed and maintained as a leisure amenity by South Somerset District Council. The route derives its name from John Leland who was a 16th century scholar, priest, Latin poet and antiquary. Leland led an interesting life. His story takes us back to a time where all education was in the hands of the religious houses and royal patronage was a key factor in securing a high income.

John Leland was born on September 13th 1503 in London. He was educated at St Paul's School and Christ's College, Cambridge. After graduation Leland returned to London and became tutor to the son of the Duke of Norfolk. Following the death of the Duke, King Henry VIII sent Leland to Oxford where he became a Fellow of All Souls College. John Leland also spent some time in France where he befriended many of the continent's leading scholars. While he was in France Leland took care to ensure that he kept himself well acquainted with the politics of the English royal court. During this time he developed a particularly close relationship with Thomas Wolsey.

When Wolsey's star began to wane with the King, Leland successfully sought the patronage of Thomas Cromwell. The support of this influential courtier made a significant difference to the rise in the fortunes of John Leland. He was appointed a chaplain to Henry VIII and from there he was granted a further four benefices. Only a short while after that John Leland was appointed Prebendary of Wilton Abbey. In 1533 Leland also managed to secure the privilege of writing the poems for the pageant of Anne Boleyn at her wedding to King Henry.

As a reward for the contribution to the wedding festivities King Henry appointed John Leland with a charter to use, examine and catalogue all of the books in the religious houses and monasteries of England. Leland set about his task with great enthusiasm and dedication, travelling up and down the country to compile comprehensive lists of books. His work became particularly important during the Dissolution of the Monasteries because it facilitated bringing together the various collections of important books from the Institutions so that they could be stored in the Royal Libraries and Cathedral libraries.

Leland's work on the books was a mere precursor to his greatest work, which became known as the "Itinerary". He persuaded King Henry to commission him to travel all over the country to record the topography and antiquaries of England. John Leland made detailed notes on everything he found throughout the Kingdom, making many long journeys between 1535 and 1543.

John Leland presented a shortened version of his notes to the King as a New Year gift at the end of 1544. Incredibly the full notes were not published in detail until the 18th century. Possibly even more incredibly the updated versions of the book are still in print today! To obtain a copy simply type "John Leland Itinerary" into Amazon.co.uk.

The itinerary is one of the few records that exist which describe the geography and antiquaries of England during the Middle Ages. This makes Leland's work an important contribution to our understanding of those times.

John Leland was both a religious and patriotic man. This came very much to the fore with his interest in Arthurian legend. He firmly believed in the tales of Arthur spreading goodness and Christianity throughout England. He would never miss the opportunity to promote the stories of King Arthur whenever possible. When Leland first saw the large hill fort at South Cadbury he immediately declared that this must be the site of Camelot. Very fittingly that is where this stage of my walk will finish later today.

Unfortunately John Leland was not given the opportunity to bask very long in his success. His mental health deteriorated quite rapidly to the extent that he was officially certified as insane in March 1550, aged only 47 years. He died two years later on April 18th 1552. There is a bust commemorating John Leland at all Souls College, Oxford.

Leland's tour of the West Country took place during the year 1542. The Leland Trail follows his footsteps as he travelled through South Somerset making his extensive and detailed records of the countryside.

Bruton

After two miles of woodland I emerge into the open fields once more. The Macmillan Way / Leland Trail here follows a dead straight line westwards for the next two miles to Redlynch. It makes good use of an old coaching road that connected Redlynch with Stourhead. There are excellent views to either side, and by looking back I can see the top of Alfred's Tower poking through the treetops.

The Macmillan Way takes me on a further two miles to the small town of Bruton. The town today has a population of 3,000 people. The Domesday Book of 1086 records the village as Briutone, meaning fast flowing river. The small River Brue still flows at a fair pace through the town, and is occasionally liable to flood during periods of heavy rain.

It is a former resident of Bruton who appealed to my sense of humour and provides me with a "Carry On" interlude for this part of the journey. Hugh Sexey was a wealthy local landowner who lived between 1556 and 1619. In 1599 he was appointed to the high office of Royal Auditor of the Exchequer to Queen Elizabeth I, a post he also held for her successor, King James I. On his death Mr Sexey left a fortune in trust to the people of Bruton. The Trust founded a hospital in his name in 1638 which is still admitting patients, and they also founded a school which opened in 1891. The school is now an Academy, taking both boarders and local children.

At this point you may be starting to snigger and thinking to yourself, "Surely he is not going to tell us that they have a Sexey Hospital? Oh indeed I am. Images of a young Barbara Windsor in a nurse's uniform haunt me as I walk through the town. All an amusing play on words for me, but I will bet that the local health workers get heartily sick of hearing it.

Coming out of Bruton there is a distant view of Glastonbury Tor to the north west. The Tor is a distinctive round hill standing at 518 feet (158 metres). It has a great prominence, with 476 feet (145 metres) from base to summit. In the days of our ancient ancestors the plain on which it stands would have been wet fenland and the hill would have risen up out of the marshes like a mountain island. You can understand how our forebears thought that this gave the hill some mystical properties.

The mystical elements of Glastonbury Tor are further enhanced by the theory that it stands at the intersection of two ley-lines. The St.Michaelos Ley-line is one of the most important to Pagans. The line enters England at St.Michael's Mount, Penzance and follows a straight line through Glastonbury Tor, Avebury Circle in Wiltshire, Bury St Edmunds, Suffolk and onwards around the globe. The intersecting line is the St.Mary Line and where they cross is alleged to create a vortex of energy.

In Celtic Mythology the Tor was the home of Gwyn ap Nudd, Lord of the Underworld and King of the Fairies. More familiarly to ourselves Glastonbury was known to the Ancient Britons as Ynys yr Afalon (Isle of Avalon) and is allegedly the Avalon of Arthurian legend where Arthur and his wife Guinevere were buried.

The roofless St Michaels Tower is just visible on the summit. This is the remains of the second church built on the Tor. St Michaels was built in the 1360's after the previous church was destroyed in the earthquake which shook southern England in 1275.

Glastonbury Tor is now managed by the National Trust and designated as a Scheduled Ancient Monument.

While Glastonbury had great religious significance in ancient times it has a very different reputation in our current era. On the last weekend in June up to 150,000 people will descend on Worthy Farm for the Glastonbury Festival. This is the biggest music festival in Britain and has been going since 1970. That first year only 1,500 people turned up to hear headline glam-rock band T Rex. Last year it was U2 and Coldplay attracting 135,000 people to the giant Pyramid Stage. There is no Festival this year due to the Olympics, but next year there are rumours that the headline act will be the Rolling Stones.

Castle Cary

Castle Cary can be considered a relative newcomer among the many towns and villages I have encountered on the Macmillan Way. While many of the others can claim Saxon, Ancient Briton and even earlier ancestry, Castle Cary only appears in records from the Norman Conquest onwards.

The name was derived from the River Cary that flows from the foot of the steep and grassy Lodge Hill. Caer meant rock, crag or castle. In the 12th century the hill was topped by one of the largest castles in the west of England, although nothing now remains of the original stone structure. The name itself has varied over the last 900 years. At different times it has been recorded as Cari, Cary, Castra Cary, Castel Cairoc and Caricastel.

I was unable to discover exactly when the castle was built. The first recorded incident at the castle occurred in 1138 when King Stephen laid siege to it during his seemingly never-ending battle for the crown with his cousin, the Empress Matilda. Stephen actually besieged the castle twice, returning again in 1152 for a second attempt.

By the 15th century the castle had been abandoned. In a similar manner to many fortresses that were left to decay the locals raided the disintegrating walls to obtain stone blocks for their own buildings. Many of the quaint stone buildings of Castle Cary can probably trace some of their limestone blocks back to the Norman fortification.

Castle Cary developed as a market town and a centre for the wool trade. It was awarded a royal charter by Edward IV in 1468. The stone market house was erected in 1616. A speciality of the local industry was a cheap cloth known as cauri-maury that was popular among the lower social classes.

Behind the Post Office and Tourist Information Office sits the "Round House". This is a quaint stone circular building, 7 feet (2.1metres) in diameter and 10 feet (3.0metres) high, with a domed roof. Perhaps you would not have thought it was so quaint if you were unfortunate enough to be one of the Round House inhabitants. The principle use it was put to in those days was as the village "lock up" for the short-term incarceration of those whose anti-social activities upset the good citizens of the town.

Castle Cary is also situated on the "Monarchs Way", a 615 mile twisting route from Worcester to Shoreham by Sea, Sussex. This trail follows the path of the flight into exile of Charles II following his defeat at the Battle of Worcester on September 3rd 1651. The King was alleged to have spent a night at Castle Cary during his escape.

Castle Cary is a key point along the Macmillan Way. It is the point where the different section paths meet. I have travelled 244 miles from Boston and have a further 46 miles to cover in order to reach Abbotsbury. If I so chose I could take a turn to the right and follow the Macmillan Way West and trudge 102 Miles to Barnstaple on the North Devon Coast. Why do the different Macmillan Ways meet at this spot? There is a reason for everything. In this case it is that Castle Cary was the home town of Douglas Macmillan.

Douglas Macmillan

Douglas Macmillan was the founder of the Macmillan Cancer Support which is where all of the sponsorship money I have collected for this walk will be donated.

Douglas was born in Castle Cary on 10th August 1884. His parents were William (1844 to 1911) and Emily (1843 to 1937).

Macmillan was educated at Sexey's School, Bruton between 1894 and 1897. He would have walked to school along the very route that I myself have travelled from Bruton. He finished his schooling at the Quaker Sidcot School in Winscombe and then spent a further year at the Birkbeck Institute in London.

In 1902 Macmillan joined the Civil Service at the Board of Agriculture and was a respected civil servant until he retired in 1945.

Douglas was very affected by the death of his father from cancer in 1911, when Douglas was 27. He thought that there should have been more understanding and support for the illness, so he founded the Society for the Prevention and Relief of Cancer.

He needed a dogged determination to push ahead with his ideas. Bear in mind that this was three years before the First World War. Not a single health Act had been passed by Parliament, nurses were not required to be registered until after 1919 and the founding of the National Health Service was still 37 years into the future. Macmillan's aim was that patients should be able to be given comfort and support in their own homes. It was a revolutionary concept at that time.

The society which he founded developed and grew into the organisation now known as Macmillan Cancer Support. The charity now has a turnover of nearly £150 million and employs nearly 3,000 nurses.

Although Douglas MacMillan was born in Castle Cary he spent most of his life in London. There is a blue plaque to his memory on his childhood house in Castle Cary, and also further plaques on his former houses in Pimlico (London) and Sidcup (Kent).

Douglas Macmillan passed away in 1969, leaving a strong legacy that has helped millions of people and their families who have been affected by this terrible disease.

Castle Cary to North Cadbury

The path from Castle Cary rises steeply up Lodge Hill. The views from the top are tremendous. I can look down upon Castle Cary, back towards Bruton and behind those buildings to the long stretch of woodlands that I walked through earlier this morning. To the northwest there is Glastonbury Tor, now very clearly defined against the bright blue sky. On such a good day there are quite a few other people up here as well, so I have to wait my turn at the topograph in order to identify all of the more distant landmarks. The Mendips, Quantocks and Somerset Levels are all clearly visible today.

I follow the long spur to the south, enjoying the views available on all sides. The paths are clearly defined and easy to follow. A slight breeze keeps me cool as I press on towards the final stages of the day.

When I come across the little River Cam the Macmillan Way undertakes a sudden change. Instead of the wide open grassy slopes I am suddenly plunged into spinneys and hedgerows with the trickling stream darting through them. Small footbridges that would be better described as wooden planks criss-cross the river. I emerge from this maze at a wonderful mill house with a working water wheel that just begs to have its photograph taken. From here it is but an easy stroll into North Cadbury and onwards to South Cadbury.

South Cadbury and Camelot

I can see the wooded slopes of the hill long before I reach South Cadbury. The green mound rises steeply behind the village of South Cadbury. The summit stands at a height of 153 meters (500 feet).It is not the size of the hill that is important, or even the fact that this place marks the end of my wanderings for the day. This place is special.

I walk through South Cadbury, saying a fond farewell to the Leland Trail as it turns to the right on its way to the old Roman settlement of Lindinis, now known as Ilchester. I turn up the steep track by the side of the church and work my way steadily up the great hill. The path takes me through trees and bushes. The steep ascent makes me puff and blow but I am determined to get there. After ten minutes or so I finally emerge at the flat top and look at the views all around me. I gaze around in wonder.

I have arrived at Camelot.

There has been a hill fort of some description here dating back to the Neolithic Period of 3000BC. South Cadbury is a Scheduled Ancient Monument. Most of the excavation work here was carried out during the 1960's by Leslie Alcock. The archaeologist made some amazing discoveries, particularly with his dating of some of the events.

The name Cadbury is a Saxo-Brythonic hybrid word. "Cadas" means fort in Saxon and so does the ancient Briton word "bury". So Cadbury Castle could translate as fort-fort castle.

The fort covers 20 acres (8 hectares) and has four rings of earthworks surrounding the summit. Exactly why there are so many early hill forts in the south and west of England is not precisely known. There are several different theories. Holding the high ground has always been a tactical advantage for the defence. Did the tribes believe that they were more secure on the high open ground? They could certainly have seen their enemies approaching. The defenders would have cleared the slopes of trees and bushes so that there were no hiding places to enable the attackers to creep up unseen.

By 400AD the inhabitants had built up some rubble ramparts and timber-post defences.

Alcock discovered evidence of violent clashes that he dated to have occurred during the first century. This is believed now to be proof that the fort was used by the Britons as a centre of resistance to the invading Roman Legions, particularly against the Augustinian Second Legion under the command of General Vespasian. With Ilchester being a key Roman settlement only a few miles to the west then this would appear to be a reasonable assumption.

It was the discovery of the remains of a Great Saxon Hall, dated at 470 to 580 AD that really sets the interest racing away. The hall would have measured 20metres x 10 metres. The defences around it would have made the defended area of South Cadbury twice the size of any other fortification of the period. The date puts it spot on the correct time for King Arthur.

At the start of the day I set off on the Leland Trail and it has taken me to the place where John Leland claimed Camelot had once stood. That later archaeological work made discoveries which agreed with his less scientific rationale makes it even more interesting. Could Camelot have really been here?

It is at this point that we have to consider a rather different scenario. Arthur may not have existed at all. This great hero of Britain may all be a combination of wishful thinking and romanticised legend. The main evidence against Arthur is that there is no record of him in the "Anglo-Saxon Chronicles". Surely, say his detractors, such a powerful leader of the fight against the Saxons would have been mentioned at some point? There is also no mention of Arthur in the works of the Venerable Bede that were written in the 8th century. Arthur is not mentioned in any record until the "Historia Regnum Britanniee" (History of the Kings of Britain) was written during the 1130's by Geoffrey of Monmouth. This was a highly popular book of the time. It tells of Uther Pendragon disguising himself as his enemy Gualguanus in order to seduce his rival's wife Igerna. Thus was Arthur conceived and born at Tintagel. Arthur then went on to secure his kingdom from the hostile advances of the Saxons with the assistance of his trusty Knights of the Round Table.

The legend of Arthur was further enhanced by "La Morte d'Arthur" written by Sir Thomas Malory in 1470 and widely published by William Caxton in 1485. This is where almost all of the romantic tales of Lancelot and Guinevere, Merlin, Gawain, The Quest for the Holy Grail and the great sword Excalibur come from.

So was Arthur real or a figment of romantic fiction? If Arthur was genuinely the King of the Britons then he would have required fortifications at the eastern end of Dumnonia (ancient Devon) to prevent the Saxons spreading to the west. So there is a logistical reason that he would have required a military presence here if he had existed.

There is one more thing to consider. The final battle between Arthur and Mordred is alleged to have occurred in AD537. Where was it alleged to have happened? The truth is that no one really knows. In some cases it is stated as occurring at "Mons Badonis", and in other cases it is said to have taken place at Camlann. At the foot of South Cadbury Hill is the River Cam. The villages of Queens Camel and West Camel are the next two settlements along that river. Could this area once have been known as the "Cam Land"? Just saying.

There are tremendous views from up here. To the west and north are the Somerset Levels. All around me the land stretches out in a rich patchwork of fields interspersed with small woodlands and coppices. Cadbury Castle certainly provides an excellent vantage point for keeping a vigilant look-out over the surrounding area. As I sit here and contemplate the surroundings I cannot help but feel that it would be very fitting if this was the place where Arthur ruled his kingdom.

SOUTH CADBURY TO YETMINSTER

South Cadbury to Sherborne

It is another bright late-spring morning. I could really get used to this weather. The first task of the day is to complete a sharp uphill climb from South Cadbury village up to Corton Ridge. This energetic start to the day is rewarded with more excellent views of the surrounding Somerset countryside. Looking back there is a clear sight of South Cadbury Castle which looks even more significant from the south than it did when I approached it yesterday from the opposite direction.

The Macmillan Way follows the top of Corton Ridge for approximately 1.5 miles providing me with superb panoramic views. On passing through the third gate along the ridge path I enter the final county of my travels. I have arrived in Dorset.

Sherborne

Sherborne is a wonderfully welcoming little town. The walls of the medieval buildings glow warmly in the bright spring sunshine.

Many of the buildings are constructed from Ham Stone. This material has a distinctive ochre colouring and is quarried from Ham Hill. You may recall that Ham Hill is where the Leland Trail finishes after threading its way from Alfred's Tower. The Ham limestone has a coarse grain and is built up from many thin beds of gritty deposit. These sedimentary beds have a habit of weathering to different degrees with the result that the facings have a very characteristic furrowed appearance.

Sherborne town centre is a veritable pleasure to wander around. The narrow streets contain many hidden treasures, almshouses, shops, houses, not to mention a wide selection of pubs and inns. I have also been promised that I will discover the "Best Fish and Chip Shop in the West Country".

The town name has early Saxon origins. It is very straightforward. "Scir Burne" means "clear stream" and refers to the River Yeo which passes through Sherborne on its journey from the Dorset Downs to join the River Parret near Langport.

Sherborne is known for its public school. There has been a school at Sherborne since Saxon times when King Alfred was a pupil here. The present Sherborne School was founded in 1550 and has developed to be one of the country's leading Public Schools.

Sherborne Abbey

Sherborne Abbey could be considered to be the great cathedral of Dorset. It often appears at its best in the evening, with the lowering sun giving the honey coloured stone a very warm and comforting glow.

Two former Kings are buried at Sherborne Abbey. Both were elder brothers of King Alfred, Aethelbald who reigned from 858 to 860 and Aethelbert who ruled between 860 and 865.

A religious building is alleged to have existed here since a church was founded by King Cenwalh sometime in the middle of the 7th century. The Diocese of Sherborne was founded by King Ine of Wessex in 705 when the great Diocese of Winchester was divided into two. The first Bishop of Sherborne was St.Aldhelm. Aldhelm was the Abbot of Malmesbury before moving to Sherborne. In addition to his religious learning Aldhelm is considered by many scholars to be the first major man of letters in the English language. He was a poet in both Latin and Anglo-Saxon languages being particularly celebrated at the time for the quality of his poems and songs.

St Aldhelm put great energy into the early development of the Saxon Cathedral at Sherborne. At 66 years of age he was a relatively old man for those days when he was first appointed as the Abbot. Aldhelm was only to survive for a further four years but he left behind a lasting legacy in the building of the Abbey. Aldhelm was canonised as a Saint soon after his death on 25th May 709. As an acknowledgement of his prowess as a poet and musician he is recognised as the Patron Saint of song writers and musicians.

Sherborne was destined to remain as the centre of the Diocese only until shortly after the Normans invasion. The Bishop's seat was moved to Old Sarum in 1075 and a continuous line of 27 Bishops of Sherborne came to an abrupt end.

Sherborne Abbey boasts a "World Number One". It has the heaviest set of eight bells in the world. The oldest bell dates from 1787. The number of bells was gradually increased over the years to the full peal of eight. The completion of the set was made in 1934 when the tenor bell, weighing 46 cwt and 5lbs (approx 2.25 tonnes) was installed. The tenor bell chimes to the tone of B flat and was cast at the famous Whitechapel Bell Foundry in London.

There have been some controversial times during the life of Sherborne Abbey. In 998 the community of secular canons who served the Cathedral were ejected by Bishop St Wulfsin following a disagreement. Wulfsin invited monks from the order of St. Benedict to replace the expelled canons. Sherborne Abbey continued to be home to the Benedictine Order until the dissolution in 1539.

A far more contentious issue was to occur during the 15th century. The monks of Sherborne had built the Church of All Hallows that joined on to the Abbey at the West End. The intention was that this church was to be used by the townspeople instead of the Abbey. The people were very resentful at being excluded from what they perceived as "their church" and tempers simmered. Eventually the people decided that they would no longer tolerate having to beg the Abbot to use the font in the Abbey for every baptism, so they built their own font in All Hallows. The Abbot was so incensed that he sent one of his henchmen enforcers into All Hallows to smash the new font into small pieces.

The result was a full blown riot in the Abbey. Somehow a fire started on some scaffolding that had been erected to repair the roof. The ensuing blaze severely scarred parts of the stonework. Arguments between the Abbey and the people raged on. It required the Pope himself to intervene before a settlement could be reached. As ever it was the common people who ended up having to pay for the repairs. You can imagine the jubilation years later when the Abbey was taken away from the authority of the monastery. The people celebrated by tearing down All Hallows and reclaiming the abbey as their parish church.

Probably the most striking feature of the interior of Sherborne Abbey is the great fan-vaulted roof. It is one of the earliest roofs of its type in England and arguably the finest example.

Sherborne Abbey was dissolved in 1539. The last Abbot, John Barnstaple, together with sixteen remaining monks handed it over to Henry VIII. The Abbey and its lands were sold by the crown to wealthy merchant Sir John Horsey. In common with many similar purchases across England at the time the Dissolution enabled Horsey to acquire large areas of property and land at a relative bargain price. The Dissolution initiated a great transfer of wealth and power away from the monasteries and was largely responsible for the massive increase in the power of the gentry from that point onwards. It was the greatest redistribution of wealth that England has ever seen.

Sherborne Castle

Castles have been a major feature along the Macmillan Way and in Sherborne I have hit the jackpot. There are two castles here with fascinating histories.

It is always amazing how things become connected to each other. One thing leads to another which leads to another and what remains at the end is nothing like the original plan. Such could be the story of Sherborne Castle.

Let us go back to the time in 1078 when the Bishop's Seat was taken from Sherborne to Salisbury. What we were left with was one of the largest and wealthiest monasteries at Sherborne being ruled by the Bishop from Salisbury.

When Henry I came to the throne in 1100 he appointed Roger de Caen as his Chancellor and deputy. In 1107 Henry also appointed Roger de Caen as Bishop of Salisbury and Abbot of Sherborne. This combination firmly placed Roger de Caen as the second most powerful man in the land.

Roger de Caen needed to have a safe place to stay when he visited Sherborne so in 1122 he started to construct a fortified palace. The design was original, differing from the layouts of the time. It was built on a low mound surrounded by a lake for added security. The castle had four corner towers and a palace in the centre. The central area was cloistered, in the manner of the monasteries. The castle was finally was completed in 1137.

Henry I died on December 1st 1139 and England was plunged into a civil war. Stephen, the grandson of William the Conqueror claimed the throne, but there was also considerable support for Henry I's eldest daughter, the Empress Matilda. Roger de Caen gave his support to Stephen, but he had made many enemies over the years.

Those enemies were able to persuade Stephen that Roger could not be trusted with the result that he was accused of treason and stripped of all of his lands and power. De Caen died in 1139, a very bitter man.

Sherborne Castle was held by Stephen until 1149 when it was lost to the Earl of Gloucester. The fortification returned to the crown in 1183 when the ownership was forcibly recovered by Henry II.

The castle was returned to the ownership of the Bishop of Salisbury in 1355. By that time the ownership had passed to the Earl of Salisbury who was challenged over the ownership by Bishop Wyvil. The Earl elected for trial by combat. Both the Earl and the Bishop selected their representative champions and a date was set for the combat. When it came to the crunch, the Earl's champion did not show up, so returning the castle to the control of the Diocese.

Following the dissolution of 1539 the castle changed hands several times before becoming a crown property again in 1578 under

Queen Elizabeth I. Elizabeth later decided to lease the castle to one of the most controversial characters in Elizabethan England, the adventurer Sir Walter Raleigh. Sir Walter was considered to be the "Marmite Man" of his day. People either loved him or they hated him. During one of the periods when he was out of favour with the Queen Raleigh redesigned the Great Tower, changed the Gatehouse and generally updated Sherborne Castle in the style of the times. He also expanded the nearby hunting lodge, adding turrets, enlarging the windows and creating balustraded roofs.

Raleigh was arrested for treason by King James I in 1603 and the castle was once again confiscated by the crown. In 1617 King James I sold it to one of his diplomats, Sir John Digby. Sir John continued with the expansion of the old hunting lodge by adding four wings to Raleigh's previous works.

During the Civil War the Digby family sided with the Royalists and the castle came under siege. It was eventually captured by Colonel Fairfax in 1645. Cromwell ordered the castle to be laid to ruin so that it could not be used again to help the Royalist cause.

When King Charles II was restored to the throne in 1660 the ruined castle and converted lodge were returned to the Digby family whose descendants have lived at the "New Castle" ever since.

The "new castle" has been updated regularly since those days. It was extensively modernised during the Georgian era, and in 1773 Lancelot (Capability) Brown designed and built a large lake in the grounds.

The grounds and gardens are open to the public between April and October. The gardens are colourful throughout the year and are set against a delightful background of sweeping lawns and elegant trees.

Only the remnants of the Great Tower and Southwest Gatehouse now remain from the original castle. The ruins have been under the management of English Heritage since 1984.

Rest of Sherborne

Sherborne is one of those towns where you can walk around it several times and each time manage to find something new. Some buildings provide a very obvious attraction. One such example is the Conduit, a stone hexagonal structure housing a drinking fountain in the centre of the town. The almshouse of St John and St John the Baptist are wonderful examples of symmetrical architecture from the middle ages. There are many other interesting designs to be discovered around the streets. Not everything is at eye level either. Keep looking upwards to enjoy a wide variety of timbered gables, chimneys, eaves, windows, and wall adornments.

There is also what I am reliably informed is "The Best Chip Shop in the West Country". When I arrived at the "Abbey Friar" the queue was stretching out of the door but fortunately it was steadily moving forward. As soon as I was inside the door I was asked for my order. By the time I reached the pay desk it was all ready for me. The food felt steaming hot even through the layers of paper. When I opened the package outside I uncovered huge pieces of battered fish and my first introduction to the delights of "Cheesey Chips". Fantastic.

Yetminster

Yetminster stands on the delightfully named River Wriggle. The village has probably not changed very much over the past couple of centuries. Many of the rich limestone buildings have been standing here since the seventeenth century. The village has an atmosphere and appearance that I will describe as "old world charm". In short it is quite a lovely place to end my travels for the day.

The centre of the village is located away from the main road, which helps to preserve the tranquillity. I make my way to the village church of St.Andrew. A small and welcoming general store stands opposite and it is soon relieved of a couple of chilled cans of fizz. It is so warm this afternoon that the first one does not even touch the sides.

My timing is such that I have unfortunately arrived too late to witness the famous chimes of the faceless church clock. Six times every day the clock will strike the hour and then play the national anthem. Unfortunately I have missed the previous performance by about half an hour.

Yetminster is the proud host of one of the oldest street fairs in Dorset. The fair was first granted to the village in the 13th century by the Bishop of Salisbury. It is held annually on the second Saturday in July.

On a wall at Upbury Farm near to the church is a blue plaque dedicated to a historical figure from Yetminster, Benjamin Jesty. I can just hear everyone asking in unison, "Who on earth was Benjamin Jesty"?

Benjamin Jesty was one of those unfortunate historical figures whose great discovery in life has been unfairly attributed to somebody else. In 1774 Jesty was the first person to use inoculation to protect against the smallpox virus.

Benjamin Jesty was born in 1736 and made his living as a farmer in Yetminster. He married his wife, Elizabeth Notley in 1770. It was part of local folk-lore at that time that dairy maids were remarkably resilient to smallpox. They often attended to sick patients and generally showed no ill effects. Several people, including Benjamin Jesty, were coming around to the theory that there must be some relationship between smallpox and cowpox and that somehow the apparent immunity gained by the milk maids was generated through the constant handling of the cow's udders during the milking process.

Jesty himself had been infected by contact with cowpox, as had two of his own dairymaids. When an outbreak of smallpox occurred in 1774 Jesty took swift action to safeguard his loved ones. He took his wife and two young sons to a cowpox infected farm at nearby Chetnole. There he used a darning needle to transfer postular material from an infected animal into their arms by making deep scratches.

Jesty was vilified by his neighbours who were aghast at the idea of transferring animal diseases into the human body. He was even attacked at local markets for his perceived wickedness. However, after some early adverse reactions to the initial infection a remarkable thing began to emerge. Despite many contacts with smallpox over the next few years Benjamin Jesty, his wife and his sons seemed amazingly immune from the effects of the virus.

Over twenty years later in 1796 Edward Jenner began his experiments with inoculation. Jenner's researches into smallpox inoculation received far more publicity than Jesty's rural practices. In 1802 Edward Jenner's results were recognised by the authorities and he received an award of £10,000 for his discoveries. This was followed by a further £20,000 granted to him in 1806.

There were several petitions from prominent people of the time for Benjamin Jesty to be given due credit for his pioneering method. Eventually after a prolonged campaign Jesty was awarded a testimonial declaring him to have been the first person to use vaccination to prevent disease. Even today many sources will still quote Edward Jenner as the founder of vaccination techniques.

Benjamin Jesty passed away on April 16th 1816. He is buried alongside his beloved wife in the churchyard at Worth Matravers, near Swanage.

I would never have heard of Benjamin Jesty if I had not undertaken this walk along the Macmillan Way. It is true. You can learn something new every day.

YETMINSTER TO COMPTON VALENCE

Melbury House and Park

As you go through life you meet a lot of people. If you retain contact with them you never know when they may come in handy. Thus it was that Norina and I spent a happy evening with Paul and Pauline Chesterman, one time economic migrants to North Oxfordshire but now returned back home to their beloved Dorset.

Paul is a passionate ambassador for all things "West Country" from Adge Cutler to Yeovil Football Club. If you can imagine the sort of bloke who can succeed in persuading a bar full of cynical South Midlanders to drink scrumpy and then go and watch him perform with the local Morris Dancers you will have some idea of what I mean.

We spent last night avidly devouring the delights of the "Best Chip Shop in Dorset", trying to sample every real ale available in the "Digby Tap" (yes, Paul insists that it is definitely the best pub in the west), followed by a few more sherbets in his local at Nether Compton. Fortunately we had a driver.

I also had a walking companion for today. Paul should think himself lucky. I only talked him into walking a few miles for a good cause. He made me watch Morris Dancers!

Today involves a lot of walking across agricultural countryside. There is not a great deal in the way of new interesting things to see, particularly after three weeks of almost continuous countryside walking. One cow looks very much like another. It will be a nice change to be able to have a chat along the way.

I have been looking forward to the walk through Melbury Park, and particularly Melbury House. The reason for this is nothing to do with any beauty that it undoubtedly possesses but lays in the name.

Aficionados of that great hotelier Basil Fawlty will recall the episode entitled "A Touch of Class". In this classic Basil wants to attract the aristocracy to his hotel and places overstated flowery advertisements in the posh magazines while at the same time insisting to Sybil that they will no longer have to tolerate the "riff raff". A guest duly arrives at reception claiming to be Lord Melbury and Basil immediately fawns all over him. Every other guest is pushed aside to give his lordship every conceivable benefit.

Chaos follows as it becomes clear to everyone else that Melbury is a confidence trickster engaged on a series of scams. He is also trying to hoodwink Basil by bouncing cheques with the sycophantic hotelier. When the miscreant is finally unmasked an enraged Fawlty erupts in anger and violence with the result that the genuine aristocratic guests leave the hotel.

The prospect of a potential meeting a real-life Lord Melbury provides a great lift for the start of the day.

The park is splendid. It is a classic deer park with a straight-as-an-arrow road leading up to Melbury House. There are many notices along the road side instructing us not to feed the deer. Chance would be a fine thing. There are no deer to be seen today. The local inhabitants must be keeping themselves well and truly hidden amongst the surrounding trees.

Melbury House dates from the 16th century. The house has an unusual feature in the hexagonal central tower rising above the rooftop. The balustrades roof must provide extensive views across the park.

Unfortunately for my wishful fantasies Paul informs me that the owner of the estate holds the title of Earl of Ilchester and not Lord Melbury. Still, it was fun while the thought was there.

Morris Dancing

Everything has its price, and in this case the cost of a day's walking with one of the West Country's finest is to be on the receiving end of a history lesson in Morris Dancing. On the basis that every day brings the opportunity to learn something new here we go.

Despite common beliefs to the contrary, Morris Dancing does not have pagan origins going back to the years when we daubed ourselves with woad and moaned incessantly about the level of illegal immigrants from the Roman Empire. The origins are far more recent, and in all probability not even English. The first written reference in England was made in 1448 when the Goldsmith's Company of London paid seven shillings to a group of Morris Dancers for entertaining them.

The term "morris" itself is very probably a corruption from "moorish", relating to the Moors of North Africa. This form of dancing is most likely to have originated from Spain and Italy to celebrate victories against the Moors invaders. There was a Spanish dance known as the "mouresca" which used swords as an embellishment. This dance celebrated the victory of driving the Moors from Spain. There are records of the "mouresca" being danced at the court of King Henry VII in 1494.

Whatever its origins Morris Dancing became very popular in the villages of England during the 16th century. It was a very common form of entertainment at the Witsun holiday time, which is possibly where all of the connections with spring and fertility started to develop. In 1600 the celebrated Shakespearean actor William Kemp famously morris danced all the way from London to Norwich in order to win a bet.

The civil war turned out to be a real downer for the Morris Men, with the Puritans outlawing the merry-making of the typical Witsun celebrations. When the Monarchy was restored with the reign of King Charles II such puritanical restrictions were lifted and the traditional practices were rejuvenated. The dancing tended to remain very much as a minority village activity for the next couple of hundred years with the local groups developing their own styles.

The great renaissance of Morris Dancing is generally considered to stem from 1899. Cecil Sharp (1859-1924) is revered as one of the founding fathers of the English Folklore revival. It was Sharp who was mostly responsible for documenting, publicising and presenting many traditional English arts. On Boxing Day in 1899 he was staying with a friend at Headington, Oxford, when the Headington Quarry Morris Dancers arrived to entertain the householder and his guests. Sharp was so taken with the music and dancing that he recorded a collection of them, ably assisted by the group's squire, William Kimber. From this humble collection several Morris "sides" were formed across the country.

A big explosion in interest and membership occurred in the 1960's. Extra leisure time and a desire to return to more traditional activities led to a boom in morris dancing clubs. Although morris dancing had been a traditionally male pastime these teams also included women, both as ladies sides, and as a mixed group.

There are currently six predominant styles of morris dance. Cotswold is the one that we automatically think of first. The dancers are clothed in white shirts and breeches, flowered hats, bells on the knees and often using sticks. Dances are for six or eight dancers. North West style is more militaristic and processional, originally performed by workers from the textile mills. Border Morris is from the Anglo-Welsh borders and the dancers often perform with blackened faces. Longsword Morris originates from Yorkshire and South Durham. As expected from its name the dances generally feature the use of swords. Rapper is not from the American ghettos, but the villages of Northumberland and Durham. Short springy swords are used for this style of morris dancing. Finally there is Molly Dancing from the Cambridge area. In this form of morris one of the participants is dressed as a woman, unsurprisingly known as "Molly".

The music is traditionally provided by a "pipe and tabor" or sometimes a fiddle. The former is a basic type of flute or whistle played with one hand while the tabor is a small drum being played with the other. Most sides now also commonly use a "melodian" which is a form of accordion. On some occassions the music is in the form of a song. The words are sung loudly by all of the dancers. It will probably come as no surprise to you that these songs tend to be very rustic in nature, and usually have a rather bawdy interpretation.

A team of Morris Dancers is called a "side" within which there are certain members who have specialist jobs to do. Each side has a leader who calls the dances and is generally in charge of the whole thing. He is known as the "squire" and often wears a top hat. The foreman is responsible for teaching and training the dancers. The kit and clothing is looked after by the "bagman" and the "ragman". There is also the "fool" who is often dressed slightly differently to the other members. He can often be seen weaving in and out between the other dancers, seemingly being both part of the dance and at the same time nothing to do with it. To do this without actually getting in anybody's way requires great skill and practice and it is often the most talented dancer who will have this prestigious role.

So there we have Morris Dancing, varying in popularity all the way from the Middle Ages but not becoming as popular as it is today until the Beatles started to play. I have left the best thing until last. Almost all public performances take place within pot carrying distance of an open bar. So go along during the summer to an alehouse where a performance is planned and sample some pure English heritage (and watch some Morris dancing at the same time). To see my informant on all things Morris waving his sticks and jingling his bells you will need to find the Wessex Morris Men in action.

Evershot

The stages of the walk through the Cotswolds were very up and down and I was always conscious of the hilly nature of that part of the trail. Up until this point I had not been so aware of the equally hilly nature of the downs of Dorset. It was therefore with some surprise that on entering Evershot I find myself in the second highest village in Dorset. Somehow I had worked my way up to an altitude of 625 feet above sea level (190metres).

Evershot was a major inspiration to the novelist Thomas Hardy (1840 to 1928). Hardy set his best-known fictional novels in this region of Wessex. Various parts of the village were used as location settings in his works.

Nearly 150 years ago Evershot suffered from a great fire. Twenty houses were burned to the ground during the disaster on 26th September 1865.

Cattistock

The Domesday Book of 1086 records the village as Entacomestock. The current population numbers about 450.

That would at first appear to be it for Cattistock, except that here we have another one of those great little idiosyncrasies that make life worthwhile. To be more truthful Cattistock provides me with a combination of little snippets for my entertainment and delight. So, if you will, just think of what fun you could have if you combined a local food speciality with the urge for a silly sport to feature at the local fete, and then stir it up thoroughly with more than a pinch of bawdy humour.

Welcome to the wacky world of Dorset Knob Throwing.

The Dorset Knob was originally developed as a way of using up the leftover dough from bread making. Sugar and butter were mixed into the dough and then it was triple baked in a process that lasted between eight to ten hours. The result is a hard, dry, spherical savoury biscuit. It is said that Dorset Knobs make very good eating and are particularly delicious when taken with Dorset Blue Vinny cheese.

There is only one commercial manufacturer of Dorset Knobs and that is Moores Biscuits of Morcombelake near Bridport. I am told by Paul that they are only baked when "in season" which he alleged was only during the months of January and February. I thank him for this information. If I sounded sceptical it is only because I am getting to the point where I suspect that somebody may be winding me up. Paul has "previous" with this sort of thing.

The Dorset Knob Throwing competition is held on the first Sunday in May. There are strict rules and the knob must be thrown underarm while keeping both feet on the ground. It must land in a marked area 30 metres long and 5 metres wide. The record holder is Philip Germain who threw his knob a distance of 26.10 metres in 2009.

As you may have already guessed the villagers do not leave the event as simply knob throwing. The day is augmented with other competitions. Villagers can take part in exciting activities such as the knob and spoon race, knob darts, knob painting, not forgetting the inevitable "guess the weight of the big knob".

Enough is enough of this ribald humour. It reminds me of the young girl who walked into a pub and asked for a "double entendre". So the barman gave her one.

Compton Valence

Compton Valence is composed of a handful of pretty cottages in an isolated location. It is so small that I will always remember it as the place where the name is bigger than the village.

I have successfully managed to get myself ahead of the game. Compton Valence is 282 miles from Boston Stump which leaves me with only eight miles to cover before I reach Chesil Beach. The countryside is changing though. The last few miles have been more undulating than anything I have encountered for a few days. The next eight miles include three quite strenuous climbs. I am comforted by the fact that whatever lies before me must involve considerably more downs than ups because Compton Valence is at an altitude of 116 metres and I will finish at sea level.

I will be returning to Compton Valence tomorrow to start the last leg of my 290 mile walk. It will not be a lonely stroll to the finish. For this final stage I will be mob-handed.

COMPTON VALENCE TO CHESIL BEACH

The Final Day

So here I am after 282 miles and 19 days all ready to step off on the last leg of my expedition to discover the Macmillan Way.

It is a good thing that I have persevered over the last few days and become ahead of the game because I am already running late. In my defence it is not entirely my fault.

I was joined last night by a group of friends who rejoice in the sobriquet of "The Weyland Mafia". Regular attendees and supporters of charity dinners, they have raised a small fortune over the years for many good causes. A sizeable cheque will be coming my way to boost the funds raised from this venture. But first I have to finish the job.

We had all met up last night in a Weymouth sea-front hotel for dinner. At this point I would like to make it clear that they chose the hotel not me. I probably would have thought twice about choosing a hotel with a night club in the basement. You can see the difficulties that were starting to pile up. There were not many other people left in the club when we eventually called it a night.

As a consequence of the evening entertainment we were much later leaving the hotel than I would have liked. I was much relieved that everyone could still walk in a straight line.

Group photographs were taken at Compton Valence and then we all set off for Chesil Beach. There were six of us in all, Peter Luffield, Peter Jones, Jim Young, Peter and Shirley Duff, with me bringing up the rear. Four of the wives had decided to "see what was in the shops". This was not good news for my credit card but would possibly pull the shopkeepers of Weymouth out of recession in just a single morning.

We started the day with a steady walk up the hill through the woodlands of Compton Valence House. This successfully cleared away the cobwebs after the excesses of last night. It also took us up to open high ground. It was another clear and bright sunny morning with excellent visibility. Once we were up on the ridge the tower of the Hardy Memorial became clearly visible on the summit of Blackdown.

Sir Thomas Hardy

Like many others I have since spoken to I had made the assumption that the Hardy Memorial was a tribute to Thomas Hardy (1840 to 1928) poet, writer and the author of such well known novels as "Far From the Madding Crowd" (1874), "The Mayor of Casterbridge" (1876) and "Tess of the d'Urbervilles" (1891). Add in that Hardy was born in Upper Bockhampton just to the east of Dorchester and it would seem a fairly straightforward connection to make.

Well; no actually.

The memorial is dedicated to Sir Thomas Hardy, who was born on April 5th 1769 in the village of Portesham situated just to the south of Blackdown. This was the man most people will only recognise when I point out that he was present when Admiral Nelson died. This was the Thomas Hardy as in the famous request "Kiss Me Hardy".

Thomas Masterman Hardy was born to local landowner Joseph Hardy and his wife Nanny (nee Masterman). Joseph Hardy owned most of the land between Portesham and Blackdown. Young Thomas was their second son and had a fierce ambition for a career in the Royal Navy. His first experience of naval life was at the age of twelve when he set sail as a Captain's servant aboard HMS Brigane. He left within a short space of time to complete his education at Crewkerne Grammar School.

After completing his schooling Hardy resumed life at sea as a midshipman aboard HMS Hebe. Naval records show that he had never officially left the naval service. He had been retained on the books of HMS Seaford and HMS Carnatic while he was studying at his lessons.

Thomas Hardy rose resolutely through the officer levels within the senior service. He saw action at all of the major sea battles of that time, Cape St. Vincent (February 14th 1797), Nile (August 1st to 3rd 1798), and Copenhagen (April 2nd 1801).

It is as Captain of Nelson's flagship HMS Victory that he will always be remembered. The Battle of Trafalgar was fought on October 21st 1805 and Hardy will forever be pictured in most people's eyes as crouching on the deck of the Victory keeping hold of Horatio Nelson while life ebbed away from the victorious Admiral.

Nelson is reputed to have held bravely on to life until he had been assured from his trusted flag captain that the French had been defeated. Before Nelson died he was reported as saying "Kiss Me Hardy", followed by his final words, "God Bless You Hardy".

Thomas Hardy returned to Britain with the surviving ships of Nelson's fleet and continued with his naval career. He was rewarded with the title of Baronet in January 1806. In July 1816 Hardy took command of the Royal Yacht HMS Princess Augusta.

More very high ranking positions were to follow. Hardy became a Rear Admiral in May 1825 with his flagship being HMS Wellesley. He finally came ashore on 21st October 1827, twenty two years to the day after the incident for which he will ever be remembered.

Hardy was appointed as First Lord of the Navy in November 1830. He was offered the opportunity to become a Member of Parliament but continually refused all such invitations. He was a strong advocate of the need to upgrade the navy and pressed the case for the development of steam powered warships.

Thomas Hardy was knighted on September 13th 1831 as Knight Grand Cross Order of the Bath. His final position in a distinguished career was his appointment as the Governor of Greenwich Hospital in August 1834.

Hardy was married on November 17th 1807 to Louisa Berkeley, the daughter of Admiral Sir George Berkeley. Together they produced three daughters, Louisa (1808 to 1875), Emily (1809 to 1887) and Mary (1813 to 1896).

Thomas Masterman Hardy died on September 20th 1839. He is interred in the mausoleum at Greenwich Hospital, now better known as the Royal Naval College.

The Hardy Memorial was completed in 1844. It was located on the exposed hilltop to act as a navigational landmark for shipping. The octagonal tower was designed to represent a spyglass, with the eight corners representing the eight points of the compass. The tower is 72 feet tall (22 metres). The height of Blackdown is 780 feet, so the tip of the tower is at 850 feet above sea level. On a clear day the Isle of Wight can be seen from the top of the tower.

The Hardy Memorial has been in the ownership of the National Trust since 1938. At the time of writing (2012) the monument is closed following an extensive restoration. Over one hundred badly eroded building stones have been replaced and the rest of the stonework has been repointed. The memorial plaque has also been refurbished.

I found it somewhat sad that most of us only know of this particular character through three words uttered by a dying British hero. The life of Thomas Masterman Hardy was filled with so many achievements for which he is so little remembered. Perhaps my small contribution here will help to promote his memory.

Kingston Russell Stone Circle

During the course of the walk I have developed a consistent pace that could be easily mistaken for a steady plod. This comfortable speed has enabled me to keep going through all weathers and terrain to bring me to this point. The fresh walkers were completely unimpressed by this and promptly strode away into the far distance. Guess who had the only guide book, map and compass?

Goodness knows how far we walked out of our way. Time after time the leading (?) group had to be called back to the correct path. At one point Peter Jones and Jim Young had gone so far down the wrong lane that the only way to call them back was to ring them using Shirl's mobile phone.

It is fair to say that the way marking on this section left much to be desired compared to the excellent markers I had encountered earlier in Gloucestershire and Leicestershire. This was augmented by there being several different pathways criss-crossing the main route, each one inviting the unwary to venture along its welcoming carpet and away from the true line. To the cynically minded (who me?) it may have appeared that any way marks were abundant where the path was obvious and at every junction there was a complete absence of them.

I regaled my companions with all of the stories of the previous three weeks. They were all highly amused by my tales of the boggy and almost impassable bridleways that I had encountered along the way. They were all delighted that they had joined me on this bright dry day in sun-drenched Dorset. There would be no such muddy struggles for them. How wrong they were going to be.

As I have mentioned previously I had the benefit of the guidebook and map. A description of a section that we were rapidly approaching did not read well. "Enclosed path, boggy ground, overgrown in places. Despair not if things get jungly". You and I know by now what that really means. If you are not hacking your way through thorny brambles and shoulder-high stinging nettles then you will be calf-deep in gunge.

True to form such was our route through Kingston Russell. Indiana Jones was undeterred and slashed his way forward with full vigour and disappeared into the distance. After a long interlude he returned to tell us that we were on the wrong path and he had ended up in somebody's back garden! We had to go back.

For possibly the first time in the last two hours Jonesy had led us exactly where we wanted to be. The track through the jungle had emerged onto a small grassy meadow exactly as stated in the guidebook. OK, the gate did lead very close to a house garden but there were Macmillan Way markers in place to guide us over a dainty little bridge across the tiny River Bride and along a surfaced driveway to the road.

From the River Bride the path crossed yet another boggy area before steeply rising up again to more hills. While we are at it, why are these hills called downs? From my own experience they would be better described as ups! At least our route ahead was very clearly defined. A recently made stone farm track went all the way up to the ridge. We flogged our way up to the summit and behold! In front of us we could see Lyme Bay in the distance. I could see the sea! The end is in sight.

There are several tumuli scattered around this area. Tumuli are ancient burial mounds dating from the late Neolithic Age. Near to the top of the hill there is a circle of eighteen low stones known as the Kingston Russell Stone Circle. The original purpose of the stone circle is unknown. It is situated at the meeting point of five footpaths, but the question that has to be asked is this unsolvable conundrum. Were the stones placed here because it was a junction, or do the paths all come here because the stones were here first?

There is one final valley left to cross. We descend to Gorwell Farm and follow a narrow lane through an attractive woodland area before turning up a well defined path to tackle the final ascent.

It was a strange feeling standing on the high point of White Hill. Below me was the village of Abbotsbury, spread along the edge of the coastline. I could easily identify Chesil Beach, the thin spit of pebbles and shingle stretching across towards Portland. Three weeks of walking had brought me all the way from the port of Boston, diagonally across England to the South Coast.

I could clearly see the enclosed ribbon of water between the mainland and the spit known as The Fleet. It was on that piece of water that the famous bouncing bombs were tested to perfection before being so effectively deployed on the "Dambusters Raid" during the Second World War.

There are some old exposed limestone quarry workings on this hilltop. It is very hard to consider that the mineral here is the same type as the Jurassic deposits that I first encountered at Kates Bridge nineteen days ago. I can see a signpost pointing the way down the path to Abbotsbury. The others have already begun their descent. I take one more look at the village below and set off after them.

Abbotsbury

The village of Abbotsbury has a population of a little over 500. As you would expect many of the cottages and houses are constructed from the local stone.

Abbotsbury grew up around the Benedictine Abbey. The abbey was founded when our old friend King Cnut rewarded his steward, Orca, by granting him this land at the western end of Chesil Beach. The monastery was the major influence on the development of the area for 500 years until the Dissolution in 1539.

All that is left of the abbey today are some ruins near to the Church of St Nicholas. I have seen more than my fair share of ruined monasteries and castles on this trip. That said Abbotsbury does have one special building still standing from the monastic days. A splendid stone tithe barn dating from the mid 14th century. The Abbotsbury Tithe Barn is alleged to be the largest thatched building in the world.

The Abbotsbury Swan Sanctuary is well worth a visit and this is the prime time of the year to go there. There have been swans at Abbotsbury since before the Norman Conquest. The sheltered waters of The Fleet provide a natural haven for the birds. There is also an abundance of natural food to be found in the lush "eel grass" that grows in the shallows.

There are written records of a managed swannery from 1393. In those days it was the exploitation of the swans as a resource rather than conservation that was the main purpose. The meat from the swans provided the monks with food, feathers were sold for hats, and the sturdier quills were used for quality pens for the bureaucrats of the day.

There are over 600 swans at Abbotsbury with at least 150 breeding pairs. Late May and early June is the prime visiting time because that is when the cygnets hatch. If you are lucky you could see the fluffy chicks emerging from the eggs only a few feet away from the footpath. As you can imagine the car park is virtually full today.

St Catherine's Chapel

The Macmillan Way provides one final up and down before reaching the ultimate end. St Catherine's Chapel stands in splendid isolation on the summit of Chapel Hill, about half a mile outside Abbotsbury. The hill is 260 feet (80m) high. A well defined path leads up to the Chapel.

It takes a little over ten minutes for me to reach the chapel. When I have reached the walls it seems to be much smaller now that I am standing next to it. The chapel looked quite sizeable from a distance. It must be an optical illusion.

St. Catherine's is constructed from the local buff coloured limestone. The walls have heavy buttresses. At one corner there is an octagonal turret giving access to the parapet. The Chapel was built during the 14th century as a retreat from the Abbey. Monks would withdraw to the isolation of the Abbey for prayer and meditation.

St Catherine was highly venerated during the Middle Ages. In common with some of the other early saints there is a considerable doubt today that she ever actually existed. The Roman Catholic Church has its doubts as well and in 1969 withdrew St. Catherine's Day (November 25th) from its Festival Calendar.

According to the legend St. Catherine was born in Alexandria in AD 282. Catherine converted many people to Christianity and through her success fell foul of the Roman Emperor Maximus I. In AD 305 the Emperor sent his most learned scholars to visit Catherine to convince her of the necessity to include the Roman gods in her preaching. This scheme backfired in a dramatic fashion with Catherine successfully converting the Emperor's ambassadors to Christianity instead. The Emperor was enraged and executed his learned counsellors as a punishment for their failure.

Maximus then worked out a plan B. He decided that he would marry Catherine himself then forbid her to continue preaching. For her part Catherine insisted that she must preserve her chastity and remain true to her Saviour. As you can imagine Maximus was not best pleased to hear this. He ordered Catherine to be tortured on the spiked breaking wheel. The legend then tells us that just before Catherine was strapped to the horrific apparatus the wheel shattered into pieces. Now absolutely shaking with rage, Maximus ordered Catherine to be beheaded instead. The story ends with angels descending from Heaven to carry Catherine's body to the church at Mount Sinai where she was buried.

The legend of St. Catherine was particularly endorsed in medieval times by unmarried women. They would call on the Saint to help them to find a suitable husband. The young girls of South Dorset were no exception. They would walk up the hill to pray to St. Catherine. There were three "wishing holes" in the east jamb of the south doorway of the chapel. The girls would push their knee into one, and a hand in each of the others before praying for a husband.

The view from the hill is magnificent. The stone buildings of Abbotsbury are shining below, and I can identify the Swan Sanctuary a little further along the coast. The Fleet reflects the sunlight, making the shallow water glisten and sparkle in the bright spring afternoon. Beyond the shore Lime Bay is dotted with the white sails of numerous sailing boats.

Chesil Beach

Chesil Beach is a long strip of shingle connecting the coastline at Abbotsbury to the island of Portland. The beach is composed of pebbles and shingle, 18 miles (29 km) in length, up to 660 feet (200m) wide and around 50 feet (15m) in height. The stones are a mixture of chert and flint. Chert is a mix of silica-rich sedimentary rocks, often having a high fossil content. The chert varies in colour, although mostly consisting of various shades of grey there are occasional flashes of reds and greens caused by trace elements. Different degrees of oxidation of iron particles also cause changes to the hue, with some interesting patterns being sometimes seen on the stones.

There is also a consistent size gradient of pebbles along the beach. Most of the stones at the south east end towards Portand resemble the size of large Jaffa oranges while the north west end has pea sized shingle. In earlier times it was said that smugglers could land on the beach in total darkness and tell exactly where they were by the size of the pebbles on the beach.

The name Chesil derives from Old English, with ceosil or cisel meaning gravel or shingle.

Although it is often likened to a spit, researchers are now convinced that Chesil Beach should more correctly be classified as a form of barrier reef. The barrier has been gradually rolled backwards until it has joined up with the land. This is caused by current and waves continually pushing the stones up the beach. Because the stones let the incoming water pass through the gaps between the stones there is a vastly reduced backwash so pressing them into a steep ribbon gradually inching inland.

Trapped between the beach and the mainland is a long lagoon of brackish water known as The Fleet. This is very slowly silting up, but it will be many, many years before this becomes more of a problem. The Fleet provides shelter for tens of thousands of birds. Over 300 different species have been spotted here at some point. The height of the pebble barrier gives shelter from the prevailing southwest winds

The Fleet and Chesil Beach were used for artillery training during the Second World War, and as I have already mentioned the "bouncing bombs" were tested here before their use on the Dambusters Raid during Operation Chastise.

The nature of Chesil Beach was such that it would have made a good strategic landing point for the German forces to invade England during the war. To prevent it being used for such a spearhead it was heavily defended. Two rows of anti-tank barriers were erected, plus many miles of admiralty scaffold, anti-tank ditches and concentrated minefields. In addition there are pill boxes at regular intervals.

The Final Steps

At first I could not see the end point of the Macmillan Way. Coming down from Chapel Hill the beach was obscured by hedges. The signs also seemed to have performed a vanishing act. Surely there is not going to be a navigation problem so close to the end?

I need not have worried. A sign said that we were now on the South Coast Path and a sudden twist to the right brought me on to the beach. Gosh, the stones were warm in this sun! It was suddenly very heavy going as my boots sank into the pebbles on every step. Suddenly there it was; the footbridge leading onto the beach proper. There were people who I recognised waiting for me on the other side.

I could not stop here. There was still another hundred yards or so to the sea and I had to see the job through to the very end before finally turning at the water's edge and walking back up the beach.

Then I heard someone say those magic words that lifted my spirits right up and made it all worthwhile. "I think you deserve a pint......."

ACKNOWLEDGEMENTS

There are many people without whose contribution and support the walk and charity donations would not have been possible.

As ever these are led by Norina, dearly beloved wife, transport manager, B&B reservation supervisor, packed lunch maker and constant pillar of support.

Jenny and Rod Davidson at the MacMillan Ways Association for all of their guidance and information.

Members of "The Weyland Mafia", Peter and Shirley Duff, Peter and Els Lindfield, Peter and Gill Jones, Jim and Sue Young. Thanks for all of your support on the last leg and for your fundraising donations.

Nigel Davis for walking the Chipping Warden to Epwell section with me and to his wife Carole for supplying the transport for the day.

Paul and Pauline Chesterman for all of their assistance and guidance in the Sherborne area and for introducing me to "The Best Chip Shop in the West Country".

Sarah Rawnsley at MacMillan Cancer Support for all the assistance with gathering collecting tins, t-shirts and other promotional items.

Gail Walker for arranging additional corporate sponsorship and acting as a collection point for cash donations.

All of those many people whose generous donations enabled me to raise over £3,500 for MacMillan Cancer Support.

Anyone who was in the locality of the MacMillan Way during May 2012 and provided a chubby middle-aged bald man with any of the numerous snippets of information that I have included in this book.

Finally my thanks to you for buying this book. All profits are donated to MacMillan Cancer Support.

USEFUL REFERENCES

During the walk and research many references were taken into consideration. These included guidebooks, fact sheets, information boards and general information sheets. Many tales were given by local people, tour guides, National Trust guides that are too numerous to list.

The major references are listed below should you wish to investigate a place in more detail.

MACMILLAN CANCER SUPPORT   www.macmillan.org.uk

GUIDEBOOK and MAPS
The MacMillan Way Guidebook   MacMillan Way Association
Ordnance Survey Landranger Maps   131, 141, 152, 151, 163,
173,183, 194

RECOMMENDED REFERENCES
British History   www.british-history.ac.uk
Cotswolds   www.cotswolds.info
English Heritage   www.english-heritage.org.uk
MacMillan Way Association   www.macmillanway.org
National Trust   www.nationaltrust.org.uk

GENERAL REFERENCES
Britannia   www.britannia.com
Calendar Customs   www.calendarcustoms.com
Castles   www.theenglishcastle.co.uk
Churches Conservation Trust   www.visitchurches.org.uk
Cotswolds   www.cotswolds.info
Dorset   www.dorsets.co.uk
Landmark Trust   www.landmarktrust.org.uk
Lincolnshire Trust   www.lincstrust.org.uk
Northamptonshire   www.northamptonshire.gov
Rutland   www.rutnet.co.uk

SPECIFIC REFERENCES

Abbotsbury	www.abbotsbury.co.uk
Aerosuperbatics	www.aerosuperbatics.com
Agriculture	www.ukagriculture.com
Alfred's Tower	www.alfredstower.info
Althorp	www.althorp.com
Automobile Association	www.theaa.com
Avening Church	www.aveningchurch.info
Avoncliff	www.avoncliffe.co.uk
Ayscoughfee Hall	www.ayscoughfee.org
Beckington	www.beckington.org.uk
Boston	www.bostonuk.com
Bradford On Avon	www.bradfordonavon.co.uk
Castle Cary	www.castle-cary.co.uk
Castle Combe	www.castle-combe.com
Chavenage	www.chavenage.com
Chedworth Roman Villa	www.chedworthromanvilla.com
Cirencester Park	www.cirencesterpark.co.uk
Corinium Museum	www.coriniummuseum.org
Cotswold canals	www.cotswoldcanals.com
Easton on the Hill	www.eastononthehill.com
Evershot	www.evershot.demon.co.uk
Eydon Kettle Company	www.eydonkettle.com
Farthingstone	www.farthingstone.org.uk
Forestry	www.forestry.gov.uk
Frampton Marsh	www.rspb.org.uk
Garden Visit	www.gardenvisit.com
Great Oxenden Tunnel	www.greatoxendentunnel.co.uk
Historic Houses	www.britainsfinest.co.uk
Holdenby	www.holdenby.com
Iford Manor	www.ifordmanor.co.uk
Kennet & Avon Canal Trust	www.kennetandavontrust.co.uk
Leicester & Rutland Wildlife Trust	www.lrwt.org.uk
Maidwell	www.maidwell.info
Mangold Hurling	www.mangoldhurling.co.uk
Megaliths	www.megalithic.co.uk
Moreton Pinkney	www.moretonpinkney.info
Nunney	www.nunney.org
Ospreys	www.ospreys.org.uk
Rollright Stones	www.rollrightstones.co.uk

Rutland Water	www.rutlandwater.org.uk
Sherborne	www.sherbornetown.com
Sherborne Castle	www.sherbornecastle.com
Sherston	www.sherston.org.uk
Spalding	www.visitspalding.co.uk
Spalding	www.spaldingnet.com
Spalding Flower Parade	www.spalding-flower-parade.org
Stamford	www.stamford.co.uk
Stow on the Wold	www.stowonthe wold.net
Tetbury Woolsack	www.tetburywoolsack.co.uk
Tunnel House Inn	www.tunnelhouse.com

Printed in Great Britain
by Amazon